THE WORLD-SYSTEM AND AFRICA

The World-System and Africa

Immanuel Wallerstein

DIASPORIC AFRICA PRESS
NEW YORK

This book is a publication of
Diasporic Africa Press
New York | www.dafricapress.com

Copyright @ Diasporic Africa Press 2017

All rights reserved. No part of this publication may be reproduced or distributed in any form or by any means, or stored in a database or retrieval system, without the prior written permission of the publisher.

Library of Congress Control Number: 2016952370
ISBN-13 978-1-937-30652-6 (pbk.: alk paper)
ISBN-13 978-1-937306-53-3 (ebook)

ACKNOWLEDGMENTS

The author and publisher thank the following for permission to reproduce the previously published essays in the collection: "How Much Change Since Independence?" in G.M. Carter & P. O'Meara, eds., *African Independence: The First Twenty-Five Years*. Bloomington, IN: Indiana University Press, 1985, 330-338; (with William G. Martin), "Southern Africa in the World-Economy, 1870-2000," in R. E. Mazur, ed., *Breaking the Links*. Trenton, NJ: Africa World Press, 1990, 99-107; "The ANC: Past and Present of Liberation Movements," *Economic and Political Weekly*, XXXI, 39 (Sept. 28, 1996), 2695-2699; "What Hope Africa? What Hope the World?" in A. O. Olukushi & L. Wohlgemuth, eds., *Road to Development: Africa in the Twenty-first Century*. Uppsala: Nordiska Afrikainstitutet, 1995, 68-84; "Construction of Peoplehood: Racism, Nationalism, Ethnicity," *Sociological Forum*, II, 2, 1987, 373-388; "After Developmentalism and Globalism, What?" *Social Forces*, 2, 2005, 321-336; "Naming Groups: The Politics of Categorizing and Identities," *Review*, XXX, 1, 2007, 1-15; "Political Construction of Islam," in K. Samman & M. Al-Zo'By, eds., *Islam and the Orientalist World-System*. Boulder, CO: Paradigm, 2008, 25-36; "A Comment on Epistemology: What is Africa?" *Canadian Journal of African Studies*, XXII, 2, 1988, 331-333; "The Evolving Role of the Africa Scholar on African Studies," in Immanuel Wallerstein, *Africa and the Modern World*. Trenton, NJ: Afrika World Press, 1986, 3-9; "Basil Davidson's African Odyssey," *Third World Review*, I, 3, 1985, 8-9; "Walter Rodney: The Historian as Spokesperson for Historical Forces," *American Ethnologist*, XIII, 2, May 1996, 330-337; "Oliver Cox as World-Systems Analyst," in H. H. Hunter, *Sociology of Oliver C. Cox*, Vol. II. Stamford, CT: JAI Press, 2000, 171-183; "Reading Fanon in the Twenty-first Century," *New Left Review*, n.s., No. 57, May-June 2009, 117-129.

CONTENTS

Introduction   i

PART I   Structural Crisis of the Capitalist World-System: Impact on Africa   1

1. How Much Change since Independence?   3
2. Southern Africa in the World-Economy, 1870-2000   13
3. The ANC and South Africa: Past and Present of Liberation Movements   23
4. What Hope Africa? What Hope the World?   41

PART II   Rise of Identity Politics: World-System Context for African Dilemmas   67

5. Construction of Peoplehood: Racism, Nationalism, Ethnicity   69
6. After Developmentalism and Globalism, What?   87
7. Naming Groups: Politics of Categorizing and Identities   109
8. Political Construction of Islam   125

PART III   Perspectives of African Thinkers   141

9. A Comment on Epistemology: What is Africa?   143
10. The Evolving Role of the Africa Scholar on African Studies   147
11. Basil Davidson's African Odyssey   157
12. Walter Rodney: The Historian as Spokesperson for Historical Forces   165
13. Oliver Cox as World-Systems Analyst   179
14. Reading Fanon in the Twenty-first Century   193

Notes   203
Index   207

INTRODUCTION

Thirty years ago, I published a collection of my essays on Africa's role in the world-economy. It was entitled *Africa and the Modern World*. Much has happened since then both in Africa and in the world-system as a whole. It seems time to try to group together another set of essays.

In this collection, I shall discuss three matters. The first is what I have been calling the structural crisis of the modern world-system. We are, I believe, in a singular transition from the capitalist system which has shaped the modern world for almost 500 years to its successor system or systems. This structural crisis will continue to go on for another 30 to 40 years. There are two possible outcomes, one better and one worse than the system in which we have been living. It is impossible to predict the outcome, but we can analyze the struggle and seek to affect it. I have written four essays, one jointly with William G. Martin, in which I seek to analyze the impact of this worldwide structural crisis on Africa.

I then turn to identity politics, a political stance that came to prominence in the last thirty years. Not unique to Africa, identity politics has become central to political struggles everywhere in the world-system. I have written four essays in which I consider the world-system context for the African dilemmas posed by this approach.

Finally, in six essays, I reflect on African thinkers' analyses of current affairs both in the world-system and in Africa.

If Africa is going to play an appropriate and significant role in resolving the structural crisis of the modern world-system, it is crucial that there continue to be a well-informed and intellectually relevant debate about the issues involved, the moral choices to be made, and the political strategies to follow. I offer this collection as my contribution to the debate. It comes from someone who is not an African but who has been involved in writing about Africa for over seventy years and who has learned much of what he claims to know from his involvement in the region.

I

STRUCTURAL CRISIS OF THE CAPITALIST WORLD-SYSTEM: IMPACT ON AFRICA

I

AFRICA AND THE WORLD SYSTEM: HOW MUCH
CHANGE SINCE INDEPENDENCE?

There is little argument among either Africans or Africa scholars about the position of Africa in the world system as of *circa* 1945. With the exception of Egypt, Ethiopia, Liberia, and South Africa—all founding members of the United Nations—the entire continent was composed of colonial territories, in which formal sovereignty lay in the hands of five European states—Great Britain, France, Belgium, Portugal, and Spain.[1] It seemed unlikely in 1945 to most people that any of these areas would be sovereign states in any near future. If one reads the most militant African statement issued in 1945, the declaration of the Pan-African Congress in Manchester, one finds imperialism denounced and all kinds of freedom demanded, but even there the word *independence* is skirted.[2]

The year 1957 is generally considered a key date in modern African political history. It is the year of Ghana's independence, that of the first African state south of the Sahara—in 1957 this distinction was still commonly made (and the Sudan was somehow considered "north" of the Sahara)—to be proclaimed independent. The road to Ghana's independence may be traced, in constitutional terms, to the Report of the Committee on Constitutional Reform in 1949 (known as the Coussey Commission). They recommended the form of local self-government under which the CPP and Kwame

Nkrumah were to come to power in 1951. If one looks at this report, one finds in it an Appendix which contains an "extract from an article circulated at the request of a member of the Committee." The article is by Felix S. Cohen and is called "Colonialism: A Realistic Approach."[3] It is a very "balanced" appraisal. On the one hand, Cohen notes the suspiciousness with which one should approach the good intentions of the colonial power.

> Colonial status is commonly justified today as a temporary institution designed to give way, in the long run, either to independence or to assimilation. The only difficulty with this theory is that, as John Maynard Keynes has observed, in the long run we are all dead. Certainly the process of terminating a colonial status in an orderly non-violent manner is one of the most difficult of political operations....
>
> Returning to our principle of political realism, we may observe that not only in determining the existence or abandonment of colonial status but also in actually carrying out a pledge of freedom, the power of government is a corrupting force....
>
> From this one may deduce that the carrying-out of a decision to relinquish power cannot safely be left to the wielder of such power.

On the other hand, Cohen expresses his doubts about the leadership of the "aborigines."

> Cynicism, however, must not be one-sided. The diseases of colonialism are not limited to those who govern. Those who are governed develop equally stubborn and serious maladies. Chief among these maladies are: (1) native toadyism, in which the native politician secures crumbs of power by adopting the usual habits of lickspittles, sycophants, and courtesans; (2) blablaism, in which natives aspiring to posts of leadership among their people, having no opportunity to demonstrate capacities for non-vocal behaviour, are appraised, selected, and bred solely on the basis of the noises that come from their mouths; and (3) noitis, in which the patient, deprived of the opportunity of action, is reduced to a position of continuous objection to the course of administration.
>
> A combination of the last two maladies generally produces a situation in which a depressed group will choose its leadership from those who most eloquently express the common distrust of the power that governs. To expect such a leadership to accept with joy promises of self-government, or of better conditions in the future, is childish. Apparently, however, Sir Stafford Cripps expected that Indian leaders

who had attained their positions of leadership by warning their people not to trust the British, these warnings have been frequently substantiated by the course of events, could turn around to their followers and say, 'The promises which the British now make are to be believed.' In all probability the only rational approach to this type of situation is the immediate transfer of new realms of responsibility to native control. Such a solution not only does away with the need for trust in promises but also inevitably modifies the character of the native leadership by instilling the habits, tests, and responsibilities of actual administration and thus replacing leaders-in-discourse with leaders-in-action.

Our realism, finally, if it is to result in a balanced judgment, must extend to the alternatives to colonialism. Do the 'Banana Republics' of Central America present a fitting ideal towards which peoples now held in colonial subjection are to aspire? Why is it that force of reaction in domestic politics (Edmund Burke and W. R. Hearst, to take two notable examples) often throw their support to independence movements of subject peoples? The answer to both questions is to be found, I think, in a recognition of the fact that economic imperialism is not necessarily dependent upon, and is sometimes even hindered by, political imperialism. Where such hindrances arise it will be to the interest of the economic imperialists to eliminate the political phase of colonialism.

Having intruded this theme of neocolonialism a decade before Kwame Nkrumah was to make it a fundamental stalking-horse of post-independence politics, Cohen concludes thus:

> Political independence, then, is not an adequate answer to all colonial problems. Recognising the distinction between economic and political dominance, we can formulate our basic problem in this way: How can we minimise the evils of political overlordship without increasing the evils of private economic exploitation?

Writing in the 1980s, I think it is easy to see that Cohen was on to the key issues, however paternalist his formulation.

Today, with a very few exceptions, all of Africa is constituted of sovereign states, members of the United Nations (and of the Organization of African Unity). As such, it is difficult to contest the assertion that relatively more African political autonomy exists now than in 1945. That is to say, it is to be sure true that in this world system, all political actors are to some extent constrained by the structural pressures of the interstate system (expressed through the power of the multiple states, but also through the power of powerful economic aggregations and of political movements). Nonetheless, it is surely the case that the power of Africans vis-à-vis others in the world system has moved along the continuum from an extremely low point to a point somewhat higher. But how much higher, that is the question.

At the same time that Nkrumah began to talk of neocolonialism,[4] Julius Nyerere proclaimed that Africa was "entering a new phase, the phase of the Second Scramble for Africa and, I believe, for Asia." He concluded this early talk with what has become quite classical North-South "dependency" language:

> Internationally, however, the picture is very different. Even between socialist countries the class divisions are getting greater. There are now not only rich capitalist countries and poor capitalist countries. There are also rich socialist countries and poor socialist countries. Further, I believe that the socialist countries themselves, considered as "individuals" in the larger society of nations, are now committing the same crime as was committed by the capitalists before. On the international level they are now beginning to use wealth for capitalist purposes, that is, for the acquisition of power and prestige.
>
> Yet whatever the internal policies may be, the use of national wealth for any purposes other than the banishment of poverty wherever it is found can have only one result. The class struggle will be transferred from a national to an international plane. Karl Marx's doctrine that there is an inevitable clash between the rich and the poor is just as applicable internationally as it is within nation states.
>
> This is the coming division of the world—a class, not an ideological division. And unless we begin to act now in accordance with our declared socialist convictions, we shall find that it is a division with capitalist and socialist countries on both sides of the conflict.[5]

What can we say about the years of independence in terms of the world class struggle? Is Africa better or worse off than in 1945? Let us not jump hastily to either the one answer or the other. It is a more complicated question to answer than it may actually seem.

The complications of assessing "improvement in situation" of a geographical area revolve around (I) the measurements one uses, (2) the other areas with which the comparison is made, (3) the time-span one analyzes, and (4) the historical trajectories one projects. Let me address these questions.

Whom and what does one measure? The whom is not an easy question to answer. The traditional measurements of developmental social science are of characteristics of a state: GDP or GDP per capita, foreign trade structure, population. If one looks at some of these figures, Africa does not look too good. Among low-income countries, Africa's growth rate of GDP, exports, or imports in the period 1965-1977 is below that of Asia. Among middle-income countries, "sub-Saharan" Africa has the lowest growth rates in that same period. If one takes GDP per capita for 1960-1990 (as projected), it is again lower than all other developing countries, the industrialized countries, and the centrally planned economies.[6]

But one can wonder if these are relevant statistics. In fact, they could hide important internal maldistributions. The improvement might be, for example, largely that of the top tenth of the population. The problem is that no one is collecting the relevant data for us to get real measures of this phenomenon. We might want, for example, comparative total household income figures (from all sources and in all forms) to measure absolute and relative rates of growth of the income of the "working strata."[7] Or we might want comparative data on real work hours per week or per year of these same working strata. Since we don't have such data, we can only use very indirect indicators of the comparative state of well-being of these strata. One such indirect measure is the degree of famine and undernourishment.

It is clear that the famines which struck primarily the Sahelian-Ethiopian band of countries in 1968-74 and then a more southerly band of countries in Africa in the last few years have been severe. There were perhaps similarly severe famines in the Indian subcontinent, in Central America, and elsewhere. But there were none such in the North. And while no one has sat down and quantified the comparison in minute detail, it is quite obvious that such unequally distributed famines must widen the gap of real incomes and real lifestyles of the working strata, North and South.

The wide literature devoted to the Sahelian famine seems to be in accord, despite distinct differences in emphasis, on the socioeconomic element in transforming drought into famine. There is agreement that, in Lofchie's formulation, "independent Africa's recent agricultural record has been one of consistent failure in food production, ... [but] one of booming success in the cultivation of export crops." For Lofchie, this is a "paradox."[8] For others, the expansion of export crops is quite directly linked to the decline in food-crop production.[9]

As for time-span, the further one goes back in history, the less is the gap in real income and real life-style between the peoples who today are located in the core of the capitalist world economy and those who today find themselves in the periphery. If the secularly widening gap did not narrow during the extraordinary world economic boom of 1945-67, it is hard to believe that it is doing anything but accentuating itself in the present long phase of economic stagnation.

The question is, has independence in any way slowed down the widening of the gap? It was of course a hope that it would in the sense that one of the main motifs of African nationalism was that if they could control the "political kingdom" (in Nkrumah's image), then economic betterment would follow. In one sense it is too early to tell. The dates of African independence hover around the year 1960. Perhaps we would do better to assess this in 2010 or even 2060. But the initial results have been sufficiently discouraging that one is tempted to infer that one of the reasons why "decolonization" was in many ways an easier process than anyone anticipated in 1945—and I do not here deny the crucial and difficult role of African political mobilization and warfare to attain this goal—may be that far-sighted policymakers in the core thought that the process of the "commodification of everything" (and therefore the process of polarization in the world economy) would proceed faster rather than more slowly under "indigenous" governments. If so, this would fit what has been the historical trajectory of the capitalist world economy since its inception."[10]

Worse yet, might it not be argued that "indigenization" is a mode of deepening and encrusting the internal formation of the standard class structure of the world capitalist system, and a way of expanding gaps internally as well as world-wide? Indeed, it might be so argued, as this seems to be what everyone knows has happened everywhere. The "waBenzi," as they are called in Tanzania, are nowhere seriously challenged, yet.

Was then the struggle for African independence a gigantic case of self-deception? No, not at all, but to see this, we must turn away from the dismal economic picture I have just been discussing and look at the *political* implications *world-wide* of the political struggles in Africa.

The nationalist upsurge in Africa (and its transformation more recently into the creation of national liberation movements) was of course part of a far wider scene. At one level, it was part of the reaction of the non-Western world to its conquest (or in a few cases its quasi-colonization) by Europe which culminated in the late nineteenth century. The rollback of "Europe," if you will, is a central cultural theme of the twentieth-century world. But it would be a mistake to see this in such limited terms. The fact is that there has been *organized* antisystemic activity within the capitalist world economy since the nineteenth century, in which one must include the rise of the social movement in Europe, the multiple Internationals, and the Russian Revolution. That all these antisystemic movements have been ambiguously antisystemic (but so, of course, has been African nationalism) does not take away from the fact that a world-wide political "force" has been in creation which has affected concretely the history of the world system and all its local units or zones in quite precise ways.

We can in some sense "measure" the overall strength of antisystemic activity in the world system as whole over time. I would argue the curve has been steadily upward for 150 or so years for the world system as a whole, if less sharply upward than many had hoped or claim. Vis-à-vis this world-wide movement, the fact that the "revolution" or the mobilization in a given country or area does not have spectacular results in terms of economic distribution or human life-style may not necessarily detract from its contribution to a cumulative *political* effect. In this sense, there is no doubt that the wave of independence movements in Africa, and the creation and maintenance of the OAU against many obstacles, must be credited with affecting the world political *rapport de forces* in a way that has weakened, if only to a small extent, the stability of the existing world system.

At this point, however, we must intrude what might be called the "ratchet" effect. No social action goes unambiguously in a single direction. Contradiction is built into all complex structures, and an antisystemic movement is a very complex structure. For one thing it inevitably brings together in a single social organization persons with a range of social backgrounds, a range of social objectives, and a diversity of degree of commitment. Secondly, creating an organization as a tool of social change is by definition double-edged, since its virtue (efficacity) also involves its vice (the tool becoming for the staff the end).

What does this mean? It means that, for all antisystemic movements, the achievement of an "interim" objective, state power, *both* undermines *and* re-enforces the existing world system. This reinforcement exists even in those cases (such as China, Vietnam, Mozambique, Algeria) when there was extraordinary mass mobilization. It is a fortiori true of the numerous situations in Africa where "decolonization" came more or less as a side effect of a struggle somewhere else.

The issue is not to make a pseudo-quantitative calculation: more undermining than reinforcing, or vice versa, in case x or y? As I said before, my clear sense is that, world-wide, there has been more undermining than reinforcing, though I would hesitate to say this was true of the African zone taken in isolation. The issue is quite otherwise. Social transformation is a cumulative process. The 150 years or so of organized antisystemic activity have collectively an impact on the social psychology of current actors.

There are three such impacts.

1. Success breeds success. If today SWAPO militants persist against great odds, it is in part because their reading of recent African history leads them to expect that per-

sistence will pay off, that sooner or later the South African regime will have to yield.

2. Success breeds disillusionment. This occurs primarily in countries which "feel" they have had their "revolution." The reality of the post-revolutionary situation is in so many ways far from the prior expectations that the "believers" grow few and the cynics abound (the cynics who profit and the cynics who withdraw into personal worlds).

3. Success breeds fear among the world upper strata. As a general social process, those on top of social hierarchies normally react to opposition in three successive ways. First, they repress. When repression no longer works, they make concessions hoping to co-opt. And when this no longer works, they adapt the old slogan: if you can't lick 'em, join 'em. Specifically, they attempt to maintain their hierarchical advantage by a total transformation of form which, however, still leaves the same con-sequence of a stratified structure.

All three consequences point to the fact that the crucial political battleground of the next twenty-five-fifty years is not interstate rivalry, or the classical forms of class struggle (private bourgeois entrepreneurs versus proletarian industrial workers), but within the antisystemic movements and the family of antisystemic movements themselves.

This is very clear in most parts of Africa, even more so than in those countries which have had more dramatic and long-drawn-out popular mobilizations. The relative political lull of Africa's post-independence governments (punctuated by politically irrelevant *coups d'état*) may not last too much longer. The question is, what is the new form that serious antisystemic struggle will take in Africa. Will it for example still give priority to the acquisition of state power by still newer organizations? I do not have the answer. But this is not an

African problem alone. Against the *de facto* "social-democratization" and welfare states of the core, we have seen the rise of a so-called New Left, which is far from having resolved its rationale or its strategy. Against the regimes of the socialist camp, we have seen multiple attempts to find alternative forms of struggle, of which Solidarność is the most salient, but is far from the definitive form. And in the peripheral areas, which are still completing the "phase" of national liberation movements coming to power, the serious question is, what next?

Let us be clear about the stakes. The alternative is not the existing capitalist world economy or a Utopian future. The existing capitalist world economy has been crumbling for some time, the result of contradictions bred by its "successes." The real question is, what comes after. The choice is between a hierarchical historical system, different from the present but still hierarchical, and a relatively nonhierarchical one. That question, it seems to me, will be determined in large part by the organizational struggles of the next twenty-five years. Africa is in many ways a key zone. For various historical reasons, Africa is less subjugated intellectually to the "universalizing" ideology of the Enlightenment which has done so much to sustain the present system.[11] It is therefore quite possible that some of the most creative organizational rethinking and reassessment will take place there. At least one can hope so.

2

SOUTHERN AFRICA IN THE WORLD-ECONOMY,
1870-2000?[12]

There can be little question of the importance of strategic issues for the peoples of southern Africa. Over the last twenty-five years the area has been racked by war. From the very moment when the southward sweep of African liberation reached the advance bastion of southern Africa, Katanga, in the Congo in July 1960, one or another part of the area has been embroiled in military struggles engaging local and extra-continental forces. Even the decolonization of Angola and Mozambique in 1975 and of Zimbabwe in 1980 failed to usher in a period of peace. Indeed, as the struggle for majority rule in South Africa escalated, and the halls of power in Pretoria became more encircled, Pretoria has organized ever-intensifying campaigns against neighboring states. The result was that interstate conflict came to be at its highest pitch ever, forestalling in the process hopes for economic improvements.

If we examine the battle for southern Africa in the post-1945 period, three distinguishing features emerge. First, the level of military and political conflict is exceptional for areas located outside the direct orbit of East-West struggles. Secondly, conflict has increasingly exhibited a transnational character, with national struggles being embedded within, or quickly engaging, regional forces and actors. Finally, as demonstrated by the forces arrayed against colonialism in the near past and majority rule in the present, Western powers have acted from the premise that local conflicts placed at risk broader regional interests. Any one of these three elements would by itself be notable. Together they offer us a composite that raises serious questions about the underlying, structural foundations of conflict in southern Africa. Why should the struggle for national liberation be so long and intense? Why have nationally contained conflicts turned out to embroil regional and world powers? And in the context of the present and near future, what are the options for different actors, given these historical patterns?

Detailed analyses of contemporary events and actors alone cannot answer these questions. We need to grasp in addition the structural conditions that underpin strategic actions, both those features that are of a long-term or enduring nature and those that are subject to change over the short- or medium-term. This leads, in turn, to a recasting of the commonplace notions of "security" and "development." If these latter concepts are to be useful, they need to be placed within the historical construction and operation of the capitalist world-economy, wherein true "development" may be defined as a struggle against the polarizing tendencies of the world-economy and the issues of "security" refer to the continuous struggle between systemic and antisystemic forces in the world-system. In order to analyze the full import of this it is necessary to grasp clearly the changing position of southern Africa within the capitalist world-economy. It is therefore useful to look at the impact of the emergence of southern Africa as a "region" has had on the trajectory of conflict and then the role of changes in the balance offerees at the level of the interstate system, including the role of antisystemic movements heretofore and their possibilities in the near future.

The stakes in the current struggle for southern Africa are high. This in itself is nothing new. From at least the turn of the century, when Britain committed a half million troops in its effort to control the area, southern Africa has engaged the attention of a worldwide cast of actors. The reasons adduced for such attention at the turn of the century match those most often proposed today, namely the value of the area's strategic resources and the existence of settler political power. With both these elements coalescing in South Africa, we are told, it is hardly surprising the level and forces currently at contest are of such depth and intensity.

While factually correct, such explanations actually tell us very little more than that the South African regime is powerful and controls considerable resources. This does not necessarily explain, for example, why struggles in the economically marginal regions far beyond South Africa's boundaries necessarily engage South Africa, independent African states, and world powers. Clearly part of the answer rests on the ability of South Africa to extend its military and economic might throughout the region. One still must ask why this so readily occurs. And even more important is the origins of this pattern: its construction, its enduring and changeable features, and its present and future trajectory.

In the opening decades of the twentieth century, there was little doubt as to the role of southern Africa in the capitalist world-economy's axial division of labor and interstate system. Incorporated into the world-economy under the aegis of British hegemony, the area as a whole rapidly became a classic peripheral area, specializing in the export of minerals and agricultural products. Processes of class and state formation moved in concert with this trend; even the creation of settler polities in South Africa and Zimbabwe was designed so as to ensure the unimpeded, trans-territorial flow of labor, commodities, and capital befitting full and open participation in the global division of labor. If South Africa was the richest prize in this network, it was nevertheless clear that the possibilities of capital accumulation in South Africa, as in neighboring territories, rested upon ever-deepening linkages with core areas of the world-economy.

Local political struggles and transformations in the world-economy as a whole in the interwar period shook up this pattern and began to alter southern Africa's role in the world-economy. The motor of these alterations was the class and national struggles that broke out in South Africa during and immediately after the First World War. Afrikaner nationalists seized the chance, and by using the nascent powers of South African state, inaugurated a process by means of which South African production processes were to be inserted in a new position in the commodity chains of the global division of labor. This process entailed a series of measures designed to alter the relational networks, binding South African economic activity to core areas, ranging from the first protectionist tariff (1925) through the promotion of core-like production (as in the establishment of one of the very first modern steel plants outside Europe and North America) to the diversification of technological sourcing among competing core suppliers. At the same time, and largely unnoticed, South African capital and the state sought to demarcate local processes of accumulation from those of surrounding peripheral areas. Imports of competing raw materials and other inputs were restricted (e.g., cattle from Botswana; Rhodesian tobacco; Mozambican sugar, cement, and labor), even while the new products of South Africa's emerging industrial sector retained access to surrounding markets.

As is readily apparent, this was not a program of autarky, but rather one of the selective management of relations with both core and peripheral zones of the world-economy, leading to a considerable enhancement of the power of the South African state. Overall, the whole process took place amidst two decisive, facilitating conditions, namely, the final decline of British hegemony and the Great Depression between the two World Wars. It was in this setting that the South African state's program became possible and successful. For southern Africa as a whole, these conditions stimulated parallel if later tendencies of disaggregation, as Portugal established the policies of the Estado Novo in the 1930s while Rhodesian settlers (stung by South African moves and advances) similarly began their own program of economic transformation. By the end of the interwar period the open economic relationships that had symbolized the early twentieth-century trajectory of die area within the world-economy had been decisively shattered.

No simple extrapolation of interwar trends into the postwar period occurred however. Curiously enough, the very success of South African advance, coupled with new world economic tendencies, was to lead to closer ties between the various parts of southern Africa. South African economic prominence by the early postwar period allowed an aggressive penetration of all southern Africa, with the novel character that it established for the first time center-hinterland relations within the area itself and not just with overseas core areas. This was a fundamentally new structural feature, giving rise to its transformation into what we have termed a "region" of the world-economy. Part and parcel of this new historical process were the conditions and alliances of the new world order established under unchallenged United States hegemony. As the world-economy entered a period of sustained prosperity, the "regionalization" of southern Africa accelerated, with South Africa slowly but surely becoming the regional base of advanced production processes implanted by foreign as well as by local capital. Meanwhile, before that, South Africa was a founding member of all the major new interstate institutions of the postwar world, which seemed to ensure the political conditions for its regional domination.

As we all know, political upheavals in the 1970s and 1980s placed in question South Africa's political domination of southern Africa. At the same time, the world-economy went into a period of economic stagnation, seriously challenging not only peripheral areas but also the semi-peripheral zones of the world-economy of which South Africa had become a stable member. The situation faced by both South Africa and new independent states in the region thus took on a very complex character in the 1970s and 1980s. At their base remained, however, the set of core-periphery relationships developed during the postwar period. These were radically different in character from those that had obtained thirty years earlier, and have proven to be more intractable to transformation than most have expected. If one could have imagined as of 1945 separate relationships between different parts of southern Africa and different core areas, the deep structural foundations of southern Africa as a region subsequently developed have precluded any simple extraction from regional core-periphery relationships that mediate ties to overseas core areas. In this context it makes little sense to speak of national development plans or bilateral security arrangements. Given the distinctive entrenchment of core-periphery relationships within the area, antisystemic struggles and hope for economic progress immediately engage regional forces. It is within this framework that we must assess the overall conditions for radical social and economic change in the contemporary period, and in this regard it is crucial to gauge the shifting trajectories of local and world powers within the current phase of the development of the capitalist world-economy.

The further political transformation of southern Africa will be directly affected by the reorganization of the balance of forces in the interstate system which is currency occurring. Regionalization of southern Africa had occurred during the period of the United States' hegemony after the Second World War and was facilitated by the enormous expansion of the world-economy which could therefore easily absorb the expanded industrial production of South Africa.

The period of the United States' full-fledged hegemony came to an end, however, in the late 1960s. It was undermined essentially by three concurrent phenomena: the rise in absolute volume of production and relative efficiency of Western Europe and Japan, which eroded many of the United States' most profitable monopolistic sectors; the rising costs of the United States' production, resulting primarily from the need to maintain internal social peace; within the United States, the erosion of the state's financial solidity caused by the enormous costs of imperialism, exacerbated especially by the Vietnam war.

By 1967, the Kondratieff A-phase of long-term economic expansion had ended and a long contraction of the world-economy had begun, one that continues to the present. In terms of capital accumulation in the world-economy, the contraction led to acute rivalry among the principal producing countries. In particular, it led to a trilateral effort by the United States, Western Europe, and Japan each to foist the immediate costs of contraction (unemployment, low profit rates, balance of payment difficulties) upon the other as well as to maneuver to control the new innovative and monopolistic sectors (e.g., microprocessors and biotechnology) which promise to be the central foci of capital accumulation in the next wave of world-economic expansion.

This acute intra-capitalist rivalry plus the internal political and economic difficulties of the socialist countries loosened considerably the structure of political alliances in the interstate system. The automatic reflexes of the 1950s and 1960s gave way to a situation in which many political battles and line-ups were ideologically difficult to explain. This is quite normal after the breakdown of hegemony, and it should be emphasized that we are only at the beginning of this process which ultimately, no doubt, will lead to new, even radically new, political alliances at the level of the interstate system.

It is therefore no accident that in the period of United States hegemony, southern Africa, which was an area relatively sheltered from the full effects of decolonization because of geographic remoteness, the hard line of the South African and Portuguese governments, and the indifference of the United States (unlike in many other areas), found itself suddenly an arena of acute antisystemic struggle. The most dramatic precipitating factor was the politico-economic collapse of Portugal which could no longer bear the social and economic costs of the struggle, given the downward conjuncture of the world-economy. It is clear that 1974 was a political turning-point for all of southern Africa. The effects of world-economic change were also felt, however, within South Africa. The growing strength of the African urban waged working class was in part the consequence of South African capital's need to remain competitive in a tighter world-economy. But this in turn was the basis of the militant trade-unionism that emerged in die 1970s, and the wave of strikes which opened the way for the resurgence of the open urban political conflict which we are seeing today.

When the president of Anglo-American Corporation meets with the leaders of the African National Congress (ANC) in Lusaka and they meet with him, when there is an Nkomati accord and when it is inoperative, when the United States oscillates between sending aid to Savimbi and agreeing to some sanctions against South Africa, we can of course explicate these developments in terms of the short-term tactics of the various actors. But one element that should not be overlooked is that it is the fact that the interstate system is being slowly restructured which conditions these actions, makes them more possible and more important. It is the fact that it is not yet clear what the political and economic line-up in the world-system will be *circa* 2000 that impels a good deal of the ground-testing that is going in.

Of course, the ANC wants to end apartheid and come to political power. But it wants then to be able to achieve significant economic transformation and expansion in South Africa itself. Whether southern Africa continues to be or not to be a "region" in the world-economy is relevant to ANC's objectives. And, of course, most of the White urban middle class in South Africa wants a minimum of real political change, but not at any price. We have seen already in other parts of the world (e.g., France in the early 1960s, the United States in the late 1960s, Portugal in the early 1970s) how behavior can change substantially when the price becomes too high. Anglo-American is afraid that change might go too far for its tastes, but it also has to plan its survival as a corporation in the conditions of those changes that seem unavoidable. And the various members of the Southern African Development Coordination Conference (SADCC) would all like the South African monkey off their back, but none wishes to remain an obscure backwater of the world-economy.

From a narrowly economic point of view, should the 1990s continue to be a period of armed struggle in southern Africa, the region risks being left behind in the economic restructuring of the world-economy. During these fifteen years, there will be a big worldwide race for the location of some of the more important economic activities of the next wave of economic expansion and, given the choice of a number of zones in which identical activities could be located, it is likely that a zone of strife will be bypassed. That is the one thing which could lead certain capital interests to favor a relatively speedy transition to majority rule in South Africa—the prospect that such a speedy transition, and only this, might stabilize economic activity in the region as a whole and thereby ensure their continued high profit levels.

In terms of the potential politico-economic realignments on a world scale, southern Africa seems to be less central (despite its mineral wealth) than the Middle East, south Asia, and the Central America-Caribbean region. In this sense, the movements of the region remain and will remain, relatively speaking, more on their own and will only achieve what they can achieve by their own struggle. There is little that will be available by default, so to speak. In the last analysis, for the five major power centers of the contemporary world—the United States, the U.S.S.R., Western Europe, Japan, and China, while there is no geographic zone to whose politics they are indifferent, developments in southern Africa nonetheless are not the top of their agenda. This is at one and the same time the region's fortune and its misfortune. That this is so is probably more fortunate for southern Africa in political terms and less fortunate in economic terms, as we move into the next round of economic expansion.

The degree to which the "regional integrity" of southern Africa can be a fortunate or unfortunate characteristic for its various peoples very much depends on how the diverse movements will relate to each other. It is doubtful that the ostensible SADCC objective—a southern Africa region minus South Africa—is feasible. Nor will a region constructed as South Africa was able to construct it in the post-1945 period be able to meet the aspirations of most of the states and peoples of the region. On the other hand, a breakup of the integrity of the region may undermine the economic hopes of a majority-rule South Africa without necessarily benefiting other countries in the region. The question may rather be: "How can the movements in the region, once the ANC is in power in South Africa, use their region's cohesiveness as a weapon in their struggle for economic transformation rather than succumbing to the constraints its structure has historically placed on such transformation?" It is clear that sensible economic maneuvering by the peoples of the region in the next period of the world-economy will require more common planning by the movements than has been the case thus far.

3

THE ANC AND SOUTH AFRICA: PAST AND FUTURE OF LIBERATION MOVEMENTS[13]

The achievement of power by the African National Congress in South Africa may mark the end of a world-systemic process that has been continuous since 1789, that of national liberation movements. Although antisystemic movements once in power failed to be liberatory, it is their very failure, and the resulting growth of independent anti-state movements, that provides hope for positive developments in the coming years.

The African National Congress is one of the oldest national liberation movements in the world-system. It is also the latest movement to have achieved its primary objective, political power. It may well be the last of the national liberation movements to do so. And thus May 10, 1994 may mark not only the end of an era in South Africa but also the end of a world-systemic process that has been continuous since 1789.

"National liberation" as a term is of course recent, but the concept itself is much older. The concept in turn presumes two other concepts, "nation" and "liberation." Neither of these concepts had much acceptance or legitimacy before the French revolution (although perhaps the political turmoil in British North America after 1765 that led to the American revolution reflected similar ideas). The French revolution transformed the geo-culture of the modern world-system.

It made widespread the belief that political change is "normal" rather than exceptional, and that sovereignty of states (itself a concept that dates at most from the 16th century) resides not in a sovereign ruler (whether a monarch or a parliament) but in the "people" as a whole.[14]

Since that time, these ideas have been taken seriously by many, many people—too many people as far as those in power are concerned. The principal political issue of the world-system for the past two centuries has been the struggle between those who wished to see these ideas implemented fully and those who resisted such a full implementation. This struggle has been a continuous one, hard-fought, and it has assumed multiple forms in the different regions of the world-system. Early on, there emerged class struggles in Great Britain, France, the U.S. and elsewhere in the more industrialized zones of the world, which pitted an enlarged urban proletariat against both its bourgeois employers and the aristocracies still in power. There were also numerous nationalist movements which pitted the people of a "nation" against an "outside" invader or against a dominant imperial center, as in Spain and Egypt during the Napoleonic era, or as in the case of the multiple movements in Greece, Italy, Poland, Hungary, and an ever-expanding list during the post-Napoleonic era. And there were still other situations in which the outside dominant force was combined with an internal settler population that made its own separate claims to autonomy, as in Ireland, Peru, and most significantly (though it is an often ignored case) Haiti. The movement in South Africa is basically a variant of this third category.

Even in the first half of the 19th century, as we can rapidly note, these movements were not limited to western Europe but included the peripheral zones of the world-system. And of course, as the years went by more and more movements were to be founded in what we later came to call the Third World, or the south. In the period from *circa* 1870 to the first world war, a fourth variety emerged, that of movements in formally independent states in which the struggle against the "ancien regime" was considered simultaneously to be a struggle for the renaissance of national vitality and therefore against the dominance of outside forces. Such were the movements that came into existence, for example, in Turkey, Persia, Afghanistan, China and Mexico.

What united all these movements was a sense that they knew who the "people" were and what "liberation" meant for the people. They also all shared the view that the people were not currently in power, were not truly free, and that there were concrete groups of persons who were responsible for this unjust, morally indefensible situation. Of course, the incredible variety of actual political situations meant that the detailed analyses made by the various movements were quite distinct, the ones from the others. And, as the internal situations changed over time, quite often the analyses of particular movements changed.

Nonetheless, despite the variety all these movements shared a second common feature as well, their middle-run strategy. Or at least it was shared by those movements which came to be important politically. The successful movements, the dominant movements, all believed in what we speak of as the two-state strategy: first attain political power, then transform the world. Their common motto was expressed most pithily by Kwame Nkrumah: "Seek ye first the political kingdom, and all things shall be added unto you." This was the strategy followed by the socialist movements which centered their rhetoric around the Working-class, by the ethno-national movements which centered their rhetoric around those that shared a particular cultural heritage, as well as by those nationalist movements which used common residence and citizenship as the defining feature of their "nation."

It is this last variety to which we have given the name of national liberation movements. The quintessential movement of this kind, and the oldest of them, is the Indian National Congress, founded in 188S and still existing (at least nominally) today. When the ANC was founded in 1912, it gave itself the name of the South African Native National Congress, adapting that of the Indian movement. Of course, the Indian National Congress had one feature that few other movements shared. It was led throughout the most difficult and important years of its history by Mahatma Gandhi, who had elaborated a worldview and a political tactic of non-violent resistance, "satyagraha." He elaborated this tactic first, in fact, in the context of the oppressive situation of South Africa, and later transferred it to India.

Whether the Indian struggle was won because of satyagraha, or despite satyagraha, is something we can long debate. What is clear is that the independence of India in 1947 became a prime symbolic event for the world-system. It symbolized both the triumph of a major liberation movement situated in the world's largest colony, and the implicit guarantee that the decolonization of the rest of the world was politically inevitable. But it symbolized also that national liberation, when it came, arrived in a form less than, and other than, that which the movement had sought. India was partitioned. Terrible Hindu-Muslim massacres followed in the wake of independence. And Gandhi was assassinated by a so-called Hindu extremist.

The 25 years following the second world war were extraordinary on many counts. For one thing, they represented the period of clear U.S. hegemony in the world-system: unbeatable in terms of the efficiency of its productive enterprises, leader of a powerful political coalition that effectively contained world politics within a certain geopolitical order, imposing its version of the geo-culture upon the rest of the world. This period was also remarkable for being the period of the largest single expansion of world production and accumulation of capital that the capitalist world-economy has known since its inception four centuries ago.

These two aspects of that era—U.S. hegemony and the incredible expansion of the world-economy—are so salient in our minds that we often fail to notice that this was the era as well of the triumph of the historic antisystemic movements of the world-system. The movements of the Third International, the so-called Communist parties, came to control a third of the world's surface, that of the "east." In the "west," the movements of the Second International were *de facto* in power everywhere, to some extent literally and usually for the first time, and indirectly the rest of the time insofar as the parties of the right fully acceded to the principles of the "welfare state." And in the "south," one national liberation movement after another came to power—in Asia, in Africa, in Latin America. The only large zone in which this triumph was delayed was southern Africa, and this delay has now come to an end.

We do not discuss clearly enough the impact of this political triumph of the antisystemic movements. Looked at from the point of view of the middle of the 19th century, it was an absolutely extraordinary achievement. Compare the post-1945 period with that of the world-system in 1848. In 1848, we had in France the first attempt of a quasi-socialist movement to achieve power. The year 1848 is also called by historians the "springtime of the nations." But by 1851, all these quasi-insurrections had been easily suppressed everywhere. It seemed to the powerful people that the menace of the "dangerous classes" had passed. In the process, the quarrels between the old landowning strata and the new more industrial bourgeois strata, which had so dominated the politics of the first half of the 19th century, were put aside in the successful, unified effort to contain the "people" and the "peoples."

This restoration of order seemed to work. For some 15-20 years thereafter, no serious popular movements could be discerned anywhere inside or outside of Europe. Furthermore, the upper strata did not merely sit on their laurels as successful suppressors of liberation movements. They pursued a political program not of reaction but of liberalism in order to ensure that the menace of popular revolt would be buried forever. They commenced down the road of slow but steady reformism: extension of the suffrage, protection of the weak in the workplace, the beginnings of redistributive welfare, the building of an educational and health infrastructure that continuously extended its reach. They combined this program of reform, still limited during the 19th century to the European world, with the propagation and legitimation of a pan-European racism—the white man's burden, the civilizing mission, the "yellow-peril," a new anti-Semitism—which served to incrustate the European lower strata within the folds of a right-wing, non-liberatory, national identity and identification.

I shall not review here the whole history of the modern world-system from 1870-1945, except to say that it was during this period that the major antisystemic movements were first created as national forces, with an international vocation. The struggle of these antisystemic movements, singly and collectively, against the liberal strategy of an iron hand within a velvet glove was an uphill struggle all the way. We may thus be amazed that, between 1945 and 1970, their struggle succeeded so swiftly and, when all is said and done, so easily. Indeed, we may be suspicious. Historical capitalism—as a mode of production, as a world-system, as a civilization—has proved itself remarkably ingenious, flexible, and hardy. We should not underestimate its ability to contain opposition.

Let us therefore start by looking at this protracted struggle of the antisystemic movements in general, and the movements of national liberation in particular, from the perspective of the movements. The movements had to organize within a political environment that was hostile to them, one that was quite often ready to suppress or constrain considerably their political activity. The states engaged in such repression both directly on the movement as such as well as on its members (particularly the leaders and the cadres), and indirectly by the intimidation of potential members. They also denied moral legitimacy to the movements, and enlisted quite frequently the non-state cultural structures (the churches, the world of knowledge, the media of communication) in the task of reinforcing this denial.

Against this massive barrage, each movement—which initially was almost always the work of small groups—sought to mobilize mass support and to canalize mass discontent and unrest. No doubt the movements were evoking themes and making analyses that resonated well with the mass of the population, but nonetheless effective political mobilization was a long and arduous task. Most people live life day by day and are reluctant to engage in the dangerous path of defying authority. Many persons are "free riders," ready to applaud quietly the actions of the brave and the bold but waiting to see whether others among their peers are joining in active support of the movement.

What mobilizes mass support? One cannot say it is the degree of oppression. For one thing, this is often a constant, and does not explain therefore why people who have been mobilized at T2 were not already mobilized at T1. Furthermore, quite often acute repression works, keeping the less audacious from being ready to participate actively in the movement. No, it is not oppression that mobilizes masses, but hope and certainty—the belief that the end of oppression is near, that a better world is truly possible. And nothing reinforces such hope and certainty than success. The long march of the antisystemic movements has been like a rolling stone. It gathered momentum over time. And the biggest argument that any given movement could use in order to mobilize support was the success of other movements that seemed comparable and reasonably close in geography and culture.

From this perspective, the great internal debate of the movements—reform versus revolution—was a non-debate. Reformist tactics fed revolutionary tactics, and revolutionary tactics fed reformist tactics, provided only that they worked, in the very simple sense that the outcome of any particular effort was applauded as positive by mass sentiment (as distinguished from the sentiment of leaders and cadres). And this because any success mobilized mass support for further action, as long as the primary objective of state power had not yet been achieved.

The passions that surrounded the reform versus revolution debates were enormous. But they were passions that divided a small group of political tacticians. To be sure, these tacticians themselves believed that the differences in tactics mattered, both in the short run (efficacity) and in the middle run (outcome). It is not sure that history had proven them right in this belief, if one looks at what happened in the long run.

If one looks at this same process of mass mobilization from the point of view of those in power, those against whom the movements were mobilizing, one finds the obverse side of the coin. What those in power most feared was not the moral condemnation of the movements but their potential ability to disrupt the political arena by mass mobilization. The initial reaction to the emergence of an antisystemic movement was always therefore to seek to maintain the leadership in isolation from its potential mass support-physical isolation, political isolation, social isolation. The states precisely denied the legitimacy of movement leaders as "spokespersons" for larger groups, alleging that they came in fact from different class and/or cultural backgrounds. This was the well-known and well used theme of the "outside agitators."

There came, however, a point where, in a given locality, this theme of the movement as being merely intrusive "agitators" no longer seemed to work. This turning point was the consequence both of the patient labors of the movement (quite often, once it had turned to a "populist" mode) and of the contagious impact of the "rolling stone" within the world-system. At this turning point, the defenders of the status quo were confronted with the identical dilemma of the movements, but in obverse form. As opposed to reform versus revolution, the defenders of the status quo debated concessions versus the hard line. This debate, which was constant, was also a non-debate. Hard-line tactics fed concessions, and concessions fed hard-line tactics, provided only that they worked, in the very simple sense that they altered the perspective of the movements on the one hand and of their mass support on the other.

The passions that surrounded hard line versus concession debates were enormous. But they were passions, once again, that divided a small group of political tacticians. These tacticians themselves believed that the differences in tactics mattered, both in the short run (efficacity) and in the middle run (outcome). But here too, it is not sure that history has proven them right in this belief, if one looks at what happened in the long run.

In the long run, what happened is that the movements came to power just about everywhere, which marked a great symbolic change. Indeed, the moment of coming to power is everywhere well-marked in general perception. It was seen at the time and remembered later as a moment of catharsis, marking the accession at last of the "people" to the exercise of sovereignty. It is also true, however, that the movements came to power almost nowhere on their full terms, and the real change everywhere has been less than they had wanted and expected. This is the story of the movements in power.

The story of the movements in power is parallel in some ways to the story of the movements in mobilization. The theory of the two-stage strategy had been that once a movement achieved power and controlled the state, it could then transform the world, at least its world. But this was of course not true. Indeed, it was in hindsight extraordinarily naïve. It took the theory of sovereignty at its face value and assumed that sovereign states are autonomous. But of course they are not autonomous and they never have been. Even the most powerful among them, like, for example, the contemporary United States, are not truly sovereign. And when we come to very weak states, like, for example Liberia, to speak of sovereignty is a bad joke. All modern states, without exception, exist within the framework of the interstate system and are constrained by its rules and its politics. The productive activities within all modern states, without exception, occur within the framework of the capitalist world-economy and are constrained by its priorities and its economics. The cultural identities found within all modern states, without exception, exist within a geo-culture and are constrained by its models and its intellectual hierarchies. Shouting that one is autonomous is a bit like Canute commanding the tides to recede.

What happened when movements came to power? They found first of all that they had to make concessions to those in power in the world-system as a whole. And not just any concessions, but important concessions. The argument that they all used themselves was that of Lenin in launching the NEP: the concessions are temporary; one step backwards and two steps forward. It was a powerful argument, since in those few cases where the movement did not make these concessions, it usually found itself ousted from power altogether soon thereafter. Still the concessions grated, leading to intra-leadership quarrels and puzzlement and questioning by the mass of the population.

If the movement was to remain in power, there seemed to be only one possible policy at this point, the postponement of truly fundamental change, substituting for it the attempt to "catchup" within the world-system. The regimes that the movements established all sought to make the state stronger within the world-economy and its standard of living nearer to that of the leading states. Since what the mass of the population usually really wanted was not "fundamental change" (which was hard to envisage) but rather precisely to "catchup" to the material benefits of the better-off (which was quite concrete), the switch in post-catharsis policies by the leaders of the movements was actually popular—provided it worked. There was the rub!

The first thing we need to know in order to determine whether a policy works is the period of time over which we shall measure this. Between instantaneous time and the Greek calends there is a long continuum of possibilities. Naturally, the leadership of movements in power pleaded with its followers for a longer rather than a shorter time-span of measure. But what arguments could they give the mass of the population for permitting them such leeway? There were two main kinds of arguments. One was material: the demonstration that there were some immediate, meaningful, measurable improvements, even if small ones, in the real situation. Some movements found it easier than others to achieve this, since the national situations varied. And it was easier to make such arguments at some moments in time than at others, given the fluctuating realities of the world-economy. There was only a limited degree to which it really was within the control of a movement in power to effectuate such meaningful, even if small, improvements.

There was, however, a second kind of argument, one about which movements in power found it easier to do something. It was the argument of hope and certainty. The movement could point to the rolling stone of the world's collectivity of liberation movements, and use this to demonstrate that history was (visibly) on their side. They thereby proffered the promise that if not they then their children would live better, and if not their children then their grandchildren. This is a very powerful argument, and it did indeed sustain movements in power for a long time, as we can see now. Faith moves mountains. And faith in the future maintains antisystemic movements in power—as long as faith endures.

Faith, as we all know, is subject to doubt. Doubt about the movements has been fed from two sources. One source has been the sins of the "nomenklatura." Movements in power means cadres in power. And cadres are human. They too wish for the good life, and are often less patient about achieving it than the mass of the population. Consequently, corruption, arrogance, and petty oppressiveness have been virtually inevitable, especially as the glow of the moment of catharsis recedes. The cadres of the new regime seemed over time to look increasingly like the cadres of the *ancien regime*, indeed often worse. This may have happened in five years; it may have taken 25 years; but it did happen repeatedly.

Still, what then, a revolution against the revolutionaries? Never right away. The same lethargy that made it a slow process to mobilize the mass of the population against the *ancien regime* operated here too. It takes something more than the sins of the nomenklatura to undo movements in power. It takes a collapse in the immediate economy combined with a collapse in the certainty that the rolling stone is still rolling. When this happens, we have had the end of the "postrevolutionary era," as has recently taken place in Russia and Algeria and many other countries.

Let us turn our look back to the worldwide rolling stone, the process within the world-system as a whole. I have already spoken of the long uphill struggle of the movements from 1870-1945, and the sudden breakthrough worldwide between 1945-1970. The sudden breakthrough led to considerable triumphalism and was inebriating. It sustained the movements in the most difficult zones, like southern Africa. However, the biggest problem the movements have had to face was their success, not so much their individual successes but their collective worldwide success. When movements in power faced internal grumbling because of less than perfect performance, they could use the argument that their difficulties derived in large part from the hostility of powerful external forces, and in large part this was an absolutely true argument. But as more and more movements were in power in more and more countries, and as the movements themselves were using the argument of their growing collective strength, the attribution of their current difficulties to outside hostility seemed to lose its cogency. At the very least, it seemed to contradict the thesis that history was visibly on their side.

The failures of the movements in power was one of the basic underlying factors behind the worldwide revolution of 1968. All of a sudden, one heard voices everywhere wondering whether the limitations of the antisystemic movements in power derived less from the hostility of the forces of the status quo than from the collusion of these movements themselves with the forces of the status quo. The so-called old left found itself under attack everywhere. Wherever the national liberation movements were in power throughout the Third World, they did not escape this criticism. Only those not yet in power remained largely unscathed.

If the revolutions of 1968 shook the popular base of the movements, the stagnation in the world-economy in the following two decades continued the dismantlement of the idols. In the period 1945-1970, the period of the great triumph of the movements, the great immediate promise was "national development," which many of the movements called "socialism." Indeed, the movements said that they and they alone could speed up this process and realize it fully in their respective states. And between 1945-1970, this promise seemed to be plausible because the world-economy was expanding everywhere and a rising tide was lifting all ships.

But when the tide began to recede, the movements in power in peripheral zones of the world-economy found that they could do little to prevent the very negative impact of world economic stagnation on their states. They were less powerful than they thought, and than their populations thought—far less powerful. Disillusionment with the prospects of "catching up" was translated in country after country into disillusionment with the movements themselves. They had sustained themselves in power by selling hope and certainty. They were now paying the price of dashed hopes and the end of certainty.

Into this moral crisis jumped the snake-oil salesmen, otherwise known as the "Chicago boys," who, with the massive support of a reinvigorated hard line on the part of the people in power in the world-system as a whole, offered everyone the magic of the market as a substitute. But the "market" can no more transform the economic prospects of the poorer 75 per cent of the world's population than taking vitamins can cure leukemia. It is a fake, and we will no doubt soon run the snake-oil salesmen out of town, but only once the damage is done.

In the middle of all this has occurred the miracle of South Africa, providing a glow of bright light in this dismal world scene. It is time out of joint. It is the 1960s triumph of national liberation movements all over again, and it occurred in the place everyone had always said had the worst situation and the most intractable. The transformation happened very fast, and with astonishing smoothness. In a way, it is an extraordinarily unfair burden the world has placed on South Africa and on the ANC. They not only have to succeed for their own sake, but for the sake of all the rest of us. After South Africa comes no other, to serve as the still optimistic mobilizer of popular forces, to be cheered on by the solidarity movements of the world. It is as though the very concept of antisystemic movements in the world were given one last chance, as if we all found ourselves at the decisive moment in purgatory before history draws its final verdict.

I am not sure what will happen in South Africa in the next 10-15 years. How can anyone be? But I do feel that neither South Africans nor the rest of us should put the burden of the world on their shoulders. The burden of the world belongs on the world. It is enough for South Africans to bear their own burdens, and to take their fair share of the world's burdens. I shall therefore reserve my remaining words to the burden of the world.

Antisystemic movements as a structure, and as a concept, were the natural product of the post-1789 transformation of the geo-culture of the world-system. Antisystemic movements were a product of the system; they of course had to be. However critical a balance-sheet we may now draw, and I fear that I have drawn such, I do not see any historic alternative that would have been better in the mid-19th century to going down the path they took. There existed no other force for human liberation. And if the antisystemic movements did not achieve human liberation, they at the very least reduced some human suffering and held the banner high for an alternative vision of the world. What reasonable person does not believe that South

Africa is a better place today than it was 10 years ago? And whom should we credit other than the national liberation movement?

The basic problem lay in the strategy of the movements. They found themselves historically in a double bind. After 1848, there was only one objective that was politically feasible and offered some hope of immediate alleviation of the situation. This was the objective of taking power in the state structures, which provided the principal adjustment mechanism of the modern world-system. But taking power in the world-system was the one objective that ensured the eventual emasculation of the antisystemic movements and their incapacity to transform the world. They were in fact between Scylla and Charybdis: either immediate irrelevance or long-term failure. They chose the latter, hoping it was avoidable. Who would not?

I want to argue that today, paradoxically, the very failure of the antisystemic movements collectively, including the failure of the national liberation movements to be truly and fully liberatory, provides the most hopeful element for positive developments in the coming 25-50 years. To appreciate this curious view, we must come to terms with what is happening in the present. We are living not the final triumph of world capitalism but its first and only true crisis.[15]

I want to point out four long-term trends, each of which is moving near to its asymptote, and each of which is devastating from the point of view of capitalists to pursue the endless accumulation of capital. The first, and the least discussed of these trends, is the de-ruralization of the world. Only 200 years ago, 80-90 per cent of the world's population, and indeed of each country's population, was rural. Today worldwide, we are below 50 per cent and rapidly going down. Whole areas of the world have rural populations of less than 20 per cent, some less than 5 per cent. Well, so what, you may say? Are not urbanization and modernity virtually synonymous? Is this not what we hoped would happen with the so-called industrial revolution? Yes, that is indeed the commonplace sociological generalization we all have learned.

This is, however, to misunderstand how capitalism works. Surplus-value is always divided between those who have the capital and those who perform the labor. The terms of this division are in the final analysis political, the strength of the bargaining power of each side. Capitalists live with a basic contradiction. If worldwide the terms of renumeration of labor is too low, it limits the market and, as Adam Smith already told us, the extent of the division of labor is a function of the extent of the market. But if the terms are too high, it limits the profits. Workers, for their part, naturally always want to increase their share, and struggle politically to achieve this. Over time, wherever labor is concentrated, workers are able to make their syndical weight felt, and this leads eventually to one of the profit squeezes which have periodically occurred throughout the history of the capitalist world-economy. Capitalists can only fight workers up to a point, because after this point too much reduction of real wages threatens to cut into effective world demand for their products. The recurrent solution has been to allow the better-paid workers to supply the market and to draw into the world workforce new strata of persons who are politically weak and are willing for many reasons to accept very low wages, thereby reducing overall production costs. Over five centuries, they have consistently located such persons in rural zones and transformed them into urban proletarians who remain, however, low-cost workers only for a while, at which point others must be drawn into the labor supply. The de-ruralization of the world threatens this essential process and thereby threatens the ability of capitalists to maintain the level of their global profits.

The second long-term trend is what is called the ecological crisis. From the point of view of capitalists, this should be called the threat of ending the externalization of costs. Here again we have a critical process. A crucial element in the level of profits has always been that capitalists do not pay the totality of costs of their products. Some costs are "externalized," that is, spread pro rata over the whole of larger populations, eventually over the whole of the world population. When a river is polluted by a chemical plant, the clean-up (if there is one) is normally assumed by taxpayers. What the ecologists have been noticing is the exhaustion of zones to pollute, of trees to be cut down, and so forth. The world faces the choice of ecological disaster or of forcing the internationalization of costs. But forcing the internalization of costs threatens seriously the ability to accumulate capital.

The third negative trend for capitalists is the democratization of the world. We have mentioned previously the program of concessions begun in the European zone in the 19th century which we have these days labeled generically the welfare state. These involve expenditures on a social wage: money for children and the aged, education, health facilities. This could work for a long time for two reasons: the recipients had modest demands at first, and only the European workers were receiving this social wage. Today, workers everywhere expect it, and the level of their demands are significantly higher than they were even 50 years ago. Ultimately, these moneys can only come at the cost of accumulating capital. Democratization is not and has never been in the interest of capitalists.

The fourth factor is the reversal of trends in state power. For 400 years, the states have been increasing their power, both internally and externally, as the adjustment mechanisms of the world-system. This has been absolutely crucial for capital despite its anti-state rhetoric. States have guaranteed order but just as importantly they have guaranteed monopolies, which are the one and only path to serious accumulation of capital.[16]

But the states can no longer perform their task as adjustment mechanisms. The democratization of the world and the ecological crisis has placed an impossible level of demands on the state structures, who are all suffering a "fiscal crisis." But if they reduce expenditures in order to meet the fiscal crises, they also reduce their ability to adjust the system. It is a vicious circle, in which each failure of the state leads to less willingness to entrust it with tasks, and therefore to a generic tax revolt. But as the state becomes less solvent, it can perform existing tasks even less well. We have entered into this vortex already.

It is here that the failure of the movements enters in. It has been the movements, more than anyone else, which have in fact sustained the states politically, especially once they came to power. They served as the moral guarantor of the state structures. Insofar as the movements are losing their claims to support, because they can no longer offer hope and certainty, the mass of the population is becoming profoundly anti-state. But states are needed most of all not by reformers and not by movements but by capitalists. The capitalist world-system cannot function well without strong states (of course some always stronger than others) within the framework of a strong interstate system. But capitalists have never been able to put forward this claim ideologically because their legitimacy derives from economic productivity and expansion of general welfare and not from either order or the guarantee of profits. In the last century, capitalists have relied increasingly on the movements to perform on their behalf the function of legitimating the state structures.

Today the movements are no longer able to do this. And, were they to try, they could not pull their populations along with them. Thus, we see springing forth everywhere non-state "groups" which are assuming the role of protecting themselves and even of providing for their welfare. This is the path of global disorder down which we have been heading. It is the sign of disintegration of the modern world-system, of capitalism as a civilization.

You can rest assured that those who have privilege will not sit back and watch this privilege go under without trying to rescue it. But you can rest equally assured that they cannot rescue it merely by adjusting the system once again, for all the reasons I have adduced. The world is in transition. Out of chaos will come a new order, different from the one we now know. Different, but not necessarily better.

That is where the movements come to once again. Those who have privilege will try to construct a new kind of historical system that will be unequal, hierarchical, and stable. They have the advantage of power, money, and the service of much intelligence. They will assuredly come up with something clever and workable. Can the movements, reinvigorated, match them? We are amidst a bifurcation of our system. The fluctuations are enormous, and little pushes will determine which way the process moves. The task of the liberation movements, no longer necessarily national liberation movements, is to take serious stock of the crisis of the system, the impasse of their past strategy, and the force of the genie of world popular discontent which has been unleashed precisely by the collapse of the old movements. It is a moment for utopistics, for intensive, rigorous analysis of historical alternatives. It is a moment when social scientists have something important to contribute, assuming they wish to do so. But it requires for social scientists as well an unthinking of their past concepts, derived from the same 19th-century situation that resulted in the strategies adopted by the antisystemic movements.

Above all, it is a task neither for a day or a week nor on the other hand for centuries. It is a task precisely for the next 25-50 years, one whose outcome will be entirely the consequence of the kind of input we are ready and able to put into it.

4

WHAT HOPE AFRICA? WHAT HOPE THE WORLD?

Anger and cynicism well up in [U.S.] voters as hope gives way.
　　　　　　　　　　　　　　The New York Times, Oct. 10, 1994

When I first set foot in Africa, in Dakar in 1952, I came in contact with an Africa in the last moments of the colonial era, an Africa in which nationalist movements were everywhere coming into existence and rapidly flourishing. I came in contact with an Africa whose populations, and particularly its young people, were optimistic and sure that the future looked bright. They were angry about the abuses of colonialism and suspicious of the promises of the colonial powers and more generally of the West, but they had faith in their own ability to reshape their world. More than anything else, they yearned to be free of any kind of tutelage, to make their own political decisions, to provide their own personnel for public services, and to participate fully in the world polity of nations.

In 1952, Africans were not alone in such sentiments and in the expectation that they would obtain their just due. The search to regain national autonomy was common to what we began to denote collectively as the Third World. Indeed, similar sentiments pervaded the peoples of Europe as well. And the general optimism was shared even, perhaps especially, in the United States, where life had never seemed so good.

Here we are in 1994, and the world now looks very different. The year of Africa, 1960, seems very long ago. The United Nations development decades seem like a wan joke. And Afro-pessimism is a new and overused word in our dictionary. In February 1994, the *Atlantic Monthly* published an article about Africa which has gotten wide publicity. Its title is "The Coming Anarchy," and its subheading reads: "How scarcity, crime, overpopulation, tribalism, and disease are rapidly destroying the social fabric of our planet."

On May 29-30, 1994, *Le Monde* put on its front page an article entitled, "The pillaged museums of Nigeria." The correspondent opens the article with this striking comparison:

> Imagine that audacious thieves succeeded in getting away with the *Auriga* of Delphi or *La Primavera* of Botticelli. Such a feat would make the teleprinters of the whole world crackle and would get at least 60 seconds of prime time on CNN. During the night of April 18-19, 1993, some unknown persons stole from the collection of the National Museum of Ife in Nigeria twelve exceptional pieces—ten human heads in terra cotta and two in bronze—which are recognized as among the masterpieces of African sculpture. More than a year later, they have still not been found; the thieves are still free and, aside from a few specialists, the rest of humanity (not to speak of the Nigerian public) do not even know this has happened.

And on June 23, 1994 a reviewer in the *London Review of Books* commented on Basil Davidson's latest book. He notes that despite the fact that, for Davidson, Africa remains "a continent of hope," even he paints a dismal picture of "the failed promises of independence." The reviewer adds that whatever Davidson "detects in the way of hopeful signs can... be very tenuous...." The reviewer then ends with this assessment of his own: "For very many Africans, at the mercy of kleptocracies, dictatorships and derailed liberation movements—sometimes of all three—there is not much solace" in Davidson's book.

So here we have it. From the wonderful days of 1957 (the independence of Ghana) and 1960 (the year sixteen African states became independent, but let us remember also the year of the Congo crisis) and 1963 (the founding of the Organization of African Unity) to 1994 when, insofar as we hear anything at all about Africa in the world press, all that the newspapers tell us is that Somalia is a land of feuding clan warlords, Rwanda a country where Hutu and Tutsi slaughter each other, and Algeria (once proud and heroic Algeria) is a land where Islamist groups cut the throats of intellectuals. To be sure, there has been one bit of wonderful news: South Africa has made an unexpectedly peaceful transition out of apartheid and into being a state where all citizens may vote. We are all celebrating, and affirming the hope that the new South Africa will not flounder. But we are also holding our breath.

What has happened in thirty years such that a continent suffused with hope became a continent described by outsiders (and indeed by many of its own intellectuals) in terms almost as negative as those used in nineteenth-century discourse? There are two things to say immediately. One is that negativity of geo-cultural description of Africa is not new; it is a return to the mode in which Europeans have regarded Africa for at least five centuries, that is, throughout the history of the modern world-system. The optimistic, positive language the world used in the 1950s and 1960s was exceptional and, it seems, momentary. The second thing to say is that what changed between the 1960s and the 1990s is not so much Africa as the world-system as a whole. We shall not be able to assess seriously anything about the state of Africa today or its possible trajectory until we first analyze what has been happening in the world-system as a whole in the last 50 years.

The defeat of the Axis powers in 1945 marked the end of a long struggle— a sort of "thirty years' war"—between Germany and the United States to be the successor hegemonic power in the world-system to the United Kingdom, whose decline had begun in the 1870s. The colonial conquest of Africa, the so-called Scramble, was a by-product of the interpower rivalry which dominated the scene once Great Britain was no longer in a position to edict unilaterally the rules of world order and world commerce.

The United States, as we know, won this thirty years' war "unconditionally," and in 1945 stood alone in the world-system with an enormous productive apparatus that had become not only the most efficient of the time but also the only one that was physically intact (untouched by wartime destruction). The story of the next quarter century was that of the consolidation of the hegemonic role of the U.S. by appropriate measures in the three geographic arenas of the world, as the U.S. came to define them—the Soviet sphere, the West, and the Third World.

While the U.S. was unquestionably way out in front of its nearest competitors in the economic arena, this was not the case in the military arena, where the U.S.S.R. was a second superpower (although, be it said, at no point matching fully the power of the U.S.). The U.S.S.R., in addition, presented itself as incarnating the ideological opposition to dominant Wilsonian liberalism in the form of Marxism-Leninism.

However, at the ideological level, Marxism-Leninism had become more a variant of Wilsonian liberalism than a genuine alternative. The two ideologies shared in fact a commitment to the basic presumptions of the geo-culture. They agreed on at least six major programs and worldviews, if sometimes they expressed this agreement in slightly different language:

1. they stood for the principle of the self-determination of nations;

2. they advocated the economic development of all states, meaning by that urbanization, commercialization, proletarianization, and industrialization, with prosperity and equality at the end of the rainbow;

3. they asserted a belief in the existence of universal values, applying equally to all peoples;

4. they asserted their faith in the validity of scientific knowledge (essentially in its Newtonian form) as the only rational basis of technological improvement;

5. they believed that human progress was both inevitable and desirable, and that for such progress to occur there

must be strong, stable, centralized states;

6. they stated a belief in the rule of the people, democracy, but they defined democracy as a situation in which rational reforming experts were in fact allowed to make the essential political decisions.

The degree of subliminal ideological accord greatly facilitated the division of world power on the terms of Yalta, which essentially were three:

1. The U.S.S.R. could have *de facto* suzerainty in a *chasse gardée* in eastern Europe (and by further amendment in a divided Korea and China), provided it in effect restricted its real (as opposed to rhetorical) claims to this zone alone;

2. the two sides would guarantee total absence of warfare in Europe;

3. each side could and would suppress groups in radical opposition to the existing geopolitical order ("leftists" in the U.S. zone; "adventurers" and "nationalists" in the Soviet zone).

This agreement did not render impossible or implausible an ideological struggle, indeed one conducted with great fanfare. On the contrary, it presumed it and even encouraged it. But this ideological struggle was to be pursued within strict limits, barring full-scale military involvement of one or the one great power outside its designated domain. Of course, a further element of this "legal separation" of the wartime allies was that the U.S.S.R. was not to expect any sort of postwar economic assistance from the U.S. in its reconstruction. It was on its own.

This is not the place to review the history of the Cold War. Suffice it to note that between 1945 and 1989, the accord (as outlined here) was essentially carefully observed. Each time its terms seemed threatened by forces outside the immediate control of the two superpowers, they managed to rein in these forces, and renew their tacit accord. For Africa, what this meant was very simple. By the late 1950s, both the U.S.S.R. and the U.S. had taken a formal position in favor of decolonization, deriving from their theoretical commitment to universal values. To be sure, it was often the case in practice that they gave covert (and even overt) political and financial support to different political movements in particular countries. The fact is however that Africa was inside the U.S. and outside the Soviet zone. Hence, the U.S.S.R. always severely limited its involvement, as may be seen both in the Congo crisis of 1960-65 and in the post-independence destabilization attempts in southern Africa in the post-1975 period. In any case, African liberation movements had first to survive on their own before they were able to get even moral support from the U.S.S.R. and *a fortiori* from the U.S.

The policy of the U.S. towards its major allies in the world arena—western Europe and Japan—was rather straightforward. It sought to aid their economic reconstruction massively (notably via the Marshall Plan). This was crucial for the U.S. both economically and politically. Economically, it was not difficult to understand. There was little point in having the most efficient economic machinery in the world-economy, if there were not customers for the products. U.S. enterprises needed an economically restituted western Europe and Japan to serve as the principal external outlets for its production. No other zones could have played this role in the postwar period. Politically, the two alliance systems—NATO and the U.S.-Japan Defense Treaty—guaranteed the U.S. two crucial additional elements in the structure it was erecting to maintain its world order: military bases across the world, and a set of automatic and powerful political allies (for a long time, serving more as clients than as allies) in the geopolitical arena.

This alliance structure of course had implications for Africa. The west European states were not only the main allies of the U.S. but were also the principal colonial powers in Africa. The colonial powers were hostile to any U.S. involvement in what they persisted in regarding as their "internal affairs." The U.S. was therefore cautious about offending its allies, especially in the period 1945-60, when the U.S. government still largely shared the views of the colonial governments that precipitated decolonization was dangerous. African liberation movements were nonetheless able to force the pace. And by 1960, the "downward sweep of African liberation" was already half completed. The year 1960 marks a turning-point, since this "downward sweep" had now reached the Congo, and thus the zone of political and economic hard-core resistance to decolonization, the settler-cum-mining zone of southern Africa. The so-called Congo crisis erupted. Within a year, there were two (in fact, two and a half) sides not only within the Congo, but among the independent African states and indeed in the world as a whole. We all know the outcome. Lumumba was assassinated and the Lumumbists suppressed. The secession of Tshombe's Katanga was also put down. Colonel Mobutu came to preside over Zaire; he is still there. The Congo crisis also transformed the geopolitical stance of the U.S. in Africa. It pushed the U.S. into playing thenceforth a direct role in Africa, deciding to defer no longer in any important way to the (ex-)colonial powers.

The scenario that the U.S. hoped would occur in the colonial world after 1945 (and more generally in the non-European world) was one of slow, gentle political change that would bring to power so-called moderate leaders with nationalist credentials who would continue, and work to augment, their country's involvement in the commodity chains of the capitalist world-economy. The U.S.S.R.'s official position was that it favored the coming to power of progressive forces that would be "socialist" in orientation. In practice, as we have already said, the U.S.S.R. was lukewarm in its support of such forces, as can be seen in their go-slow advice to the Chinese Communist Party in 1945, in their long delay in supporting the independence movement in Algeria, and in the support the Cuban Communist Party gave to Batista right up to 1959.

What neither the U.S. nor the U.S.S.R. expected was the intensity of the national liberation movements in the extra-European world at this time. To be sure, all kinds of radical nationalist outbreaks were suppressed—in Malaya, the Philippines, and Iran; in Madagascar, Kenya, and Cameroon; in multiple countries of the Americas. Even where such uprisings were suppressed, however, they pushed forward the calendar of decolonization.

And in four countries, there were extremely strong, ultimately victorious, wars of liberation that left a major mark. They were China, Vietnam, Algeria, and Cuba. In all four cases, the movements refused to accept the rules of the game, as the U.S. defined them, and as the U.S.S.R. tacitly endorsed them.

The details of each case was different, because the geography, the history, and the array of internal social forces was different. But all four movements shared certain features:

1. they imposed their arrival in power on the world-system's great powers; their strength was in the fierceness with which they pursued their political autonomy;

2. they proclaimed a belief in modernity and national development;

3. they sought power in the state as the necessary prerequisite of social transformation, and once in power they sought to achieve full legitimation by the populace of the strong state they were erecting;

4. they were sure that they were riding the wave of historical progress.

By 1965, the spirit of Bandung seemed to have conquered the world. The national liberation movements had come to power everywhere, except in southern Africa, and armed struggle had begun there as well. It was, if you will, a strange situation. Never had the U.S. seemed so in control of the situation, so on top of everything. Yet also never had antisystemic movements seemed so strong. It was the calm in the eye of the hurricane. There were early warning signals in Africa. The year 1965 saw the fall of some of the symbolic figures of the so-called Casablanca group, the group of more "militant" states: Nkrumah in Ghana, Modibo Keita in Mali, Ben Bella in Algeria. It was as well the year the Rhodesian settlers proclaimed UDI, the Unilateral Declaration of Independence. And in the United States, it was the year of the first Vietnam teach-in. In 1966, the Chinese Cultural Revolution started. The momentous year of 1968 was in sight.

Early in 1968 the Tet offensive signaled the incapacity of the United States to win the war in Vietnam. In February, Martin Luther King was assassinated. And in April, the worldwide revolution of 1968 began. Over three years it occurred everywhere—in North America, Europe and Japan; in the Communist world; and in Latin America, Africa and South Asia. The local manifestations were each sure to be different from the other. But two themes were common and thus made of these multiple uprisings a worldwide event. The first was antagonism to U.S. hegemony (symbolized by opposition to its role in Vietnam), and to Soviet collusion with the U.S. (as evoked in the theme of the "two superpowers"). The second was a deep disillusion with the so-called Old Left, in all its three major variants: Social-Democratic parties in the West; Communist parties; national liberation movements in the Third World. The revolutionaries of 1968 saw the Old Left as insufficiently and ineffectively antisystemic. Indeed, one might argue that, even more than the U.S., the Old Left was the prime villain of the piece for the revolutionaries of 1968.

As a political event, the world revolution of 1968 flared up quickly and then was extinguished. By 1970, there were only embers—mostly in the form of Maoist sects. By 1975, even the embers had been extinguished. Nonetheless, the revolution left a lasting impact. It delegitimized reformist centrist liberalism as the reigning ideology of the geo-culture, reducing liberalism to being merely one competing ideology in the arena, with strong forces both to its right and to its left. It soured people everywhere on the state as the instrument of social transformation. And it destroyed the optimism about the inevitability of progress, especially when the last avatar of such optimism, its own meteoric career, fizzled out. The mood had turned.

The events in 1968 took place at just the moment that the world-economy was entering into the Kondratieff-B downturn in which we still find ourselves today. Once again, as has happened repeatedly in the history of the capitalist world-economy, the high profitability of the leading sectors had come to an end, primarily because the relative monopoly of a few firms had been undermined by persistent entry into the market of new producers attracted by the high rates of profit and usually supported by governments of semi-peripheral states. The acute decline in worldwide rates of profit from productive activities resulted, as one could expect, in reduction of production and unemployment in the *loci* of leading sectors; consequently in the reduction of purchases of raw material imports coming from peripheral zones; further relocation of industries to semi-peripheral zones in search of lowered labor costs; acute competition between states in the core zone seeking to shift the negative burdens to each other; and a significant shift of investors from seeking profits in production to seeking profits in financial (speculative) activities.

In this particular B-phase, the two major events which brought the economic stagnation to the world's attention (but by no means could be said to have caused the stagnation) were successively the OPEC oil price rises of the 1970s and the debt crisis of the 1980s. Both of course had particularly negative consequences for the South in general, not least of all for Africa. It is worth discussing their significance as politico-economic mechanisms of adjustment.

In 1973, the Organization of Petroleum Exporting Countries, OPEC—a group that had been in somnolent and obscure existence for more than a decade—suddenly announced a spectacular price rise. Notice several things about this event. Oil prices had been remarkably low during the whole Kondratieff A-phase, when world production was expanding. Yet, it was precisely at the moment when the world-economy began to be in trouble and when producers were everywhere beginning to seek ways in which they could sell their products in a tighter market by either reducing their prices or reducing their costs that the oil producers raised their prices, and not by a small amount. The effect, of course, was to raise the costs of production of almost every industrial process worldwide, since oil is a direct or indirect component of almost all of this production.

What was the rationale of such an action? One might argue that it was a syndical action by the oil-exporting states seeking to take advantage of an economically weakened Western world to alter the distribution of world surplus-value in their favor. This might explain why members of OPEC who had politically radical governments at the time, such as Algeria or Iraq, were pushing for such action. But why would the two closest allies of the United States in the oil region—Saudi Arabia and Iran (the Iran of the Shah)—have not merely gone along but actually taken the lead in obtaining the OPEC accord on a joint price rise? And if the action was intended to rectify the distribution of world surplus-value, how is it that the immediate effect was actually to increase the amount of world surplus-value in the hands of U.S. corporations?

Let us look at what happens when you raise oil prices suddenly and drastically. Since it is hard to reduce the need for oil very quickly, several things follow. The revenues of the oil producers go up, indeed go way up. This is so despite the fact that the quantity of oil sold is reduced, since it has become so expensive. A reduction in the quantity of oil sold means a reduction in world current production, but that actually is a plus given the fact that there had been in the 1960s overproduction in the erstwhile leading sectors. Indeed, it makes more legitimate the laying-off of industrial workers.

For non-oil-producing states in the peripheral zone, for example, most African states, the oil price rise was a very severe blow. The price of importing oil went up. The price of importing industrial products in whose production oil played a significant role, which is almost all production as we have already noted, went up. And this occurred at a time when the quantity and often the per unit price of exports was going down. Of course, African states (except for a few) found themselves in severe balance of payments squeezes. The populations found themselves confronted with reduced standards of living and deteriorating governmental services. They would scarcely be content with this apparent outcome of the independences for which they had successfully struggled a decade or so earlier. They turned against the very movements they had previously supported so strongly, especially whenever they saw signs of corruption and high living among their elites.

Of course, oil prices did not rise for Africans alone; they rose everywhere, including in the U.S. It was part of a long inflationary thrust, which was generated by many other factors. What the oil price rise (itself not cause but consequence of the world economic stagnation) did was to create a big funnel channeling a remarkably large portion of world surplus-value through its cash registers. What happened to this revenue? Some of it was kept by the oil-producing states as rent and served to permit luxury consumption for a small minority, and also for a short while improved levels of income for a larger segment of the citizenry. It permitted these states to engage in infrastructural construction and arms purchases on a large scale. The latter was socially less useful than the former, especially since it would permit such spectacular wastage of lives and accumulated capital stock as the Iran-Iraq war of the 1980s. But both kinds of expenditure—infrastructure and arms purchases—helped resolve part of the economic difficulties of the states in the North, from which the goods were imported.

Still, expenditures within the oil-producing states accounts for only part of the revenue. Another large part went to the Seven Sisters, that is, to the Western petroleum corporations who no longer controlled oil production but who continued to control worldwide oil refining and oil distribution. What did they in turn do with their extraordinary profit windfalls? In the absence of too many profitable production outlets, they placed a good portion of this money in the world financial markets, fueling the incredible currency roller-coaster of the past two decades.

All this activity did not exhaust the coffers of this concentration of world surplus-value. The rest was placed as accounts in banks, primarily in the U.S. but also in western Europe. Bank profits of course come from lending the money that is deposited with them. And the banks now had huge additional sums deposited—at a time where new productive enterprise was slowing down, as compared with the Kondratieff A-phase. To whom could the banks lend the money?

The answer seemed obvious: to governments in balance of payments difficulties, which meant almost all African states, large portions of Latin America and Asia, and almost all the so-called socialist bloc as well (from Poland to Romania to the U.S.S.R. to North Korea). In the mid-1970s world banks pressed these loans upon these governments, which seized the opportunity to balance their accounts in this way and reduce somewhat the immediate political pressures of unhappy ordinary citizens. Similar loans were made even to the oil-producing states who did not need to balance their accounts but were anxious to spend quickly on what they perceived (and misperceived) as "development." These loans in turn helped the Western countries by counteracting the inability of the rest of the world to purchase their exports.

The situation in Western countries must be analyzed carefully. There are three different ways to assess what happened in the 1970s and continued in the 1980s. One is to see how the countries fared globally. Globally, their rates of growth went down considerably from the Kondratieff A-phase of 1945-*circa* 1970, although in absolute terms they of course kept growing. Secondly, one can assess them in relation to each other. Here we can see that, despite the best efforts of the U.S. (and its early advantage from the OPEC action deriving from the fact that it was less dependent on oil imports than western Europe or Japan), the U.S. economic position has declined overall in relation to western Europe and especially Japan, despite constant short-term reversals of fortune.

Thirdly, one can assess them in terms of internal distribution of the surplus-value. While it could be said that the pattern of the A-phase had been one of overall improvement of income levels and some convergence of extremes, the pattern of the B-phase has been rather one of considerable increase in internal polarization of revenue. A small percentage has done quite well, at least for a long time; we have even invented a term for them, the "yuppies." But, aside from this small group, there has been a marked increase in internal poverty, eventually a thrust down from middle-class status of a considerable group, and a decline in real income for most of the rest of the middle strata. This internal polarization has been particularly marked in the U.S. and Great Britain, but is also true of continental western Europe, and even of Japan.

A word should be said at this point about East Asia, especially since it is constantly thrown in the face of Africans as a model of successful development. Whenever there is a stagnation of the world-economy and a squeeze on profits in general and profits from productive activities in particular, one geographic zone, previously not at the top of the profit-making hierarchy, tends to do very well. It becomes the locus of considerable worldwide relocation of production, the beneficiary of the difficulties of the world-economy as a whole. In the 1970s and since, this zone has been East Asia—or more precisely, primarily Japan, secondarily its immediate rim of the so-called Four Dragons, and tertiarily (and more recently) of a series of countries in southeast Asia. How East Asia was able to become this beneficiary region is not to the point in this discussion, except for two remarks. A key role was played by governmental involvement in the construction of the necessary economic frameworks and state protection of the internal markets. And secondly, there was no way that a second zone could have achieved the same economic returns simultaneously. It could have been the case that some region other than East Asia achieved this growth, but it could not have been both East Asia and a second region. Hence, East Asia presents no relevant model for Africa in any near future.

I have spent so much time on the OPEC oil rise not because it was a key cause of economic distress. It was not; it was merely one intervening process by which the world-economic stagnation had its effect. But it was very visible, and looking at the mechanism in detail makes clearer the process. It also helps to illuminate the 1980s when the world forgot about oil prices since they came down again, if not quite to their 1950 levels. The loans to governments came home to roost in the 1980s. Loans solve balance of payments in the present, to create them down the line, as the costs of debt repayment as a percentage of national income go up. The decade of the 1980s started out with the so-called debt crisis and ended with the so-called collapse of the Communisms. They are not unrelated.

The term debt crisis appeared in 1982 when Mexico, an oil-producing country, announced its inability to keep up with debt repayments and sought renegotiation of the debt. Actually the debt crisis initially surfaced in 1980 in Poland, a heavy borrower in the 1970s, when the Gierek government, faced with debt repayment problems, tried to reduce wage levels as a partial solution. Result: Solidarność. The Polish Communist government got into trouble because it began to implement the IMF remedy for e situation without even having the IMF ask it to do this. What the IMF began to recommend to all countries in this situation (not least to African states) was that they reduce expenditures (fewer imports and less welfare for the population) and increase exports (by keeping wages low or lowering them, by diverting production from production for internal needs to whatever was sellable immediately on the world market). The weapon the IMF had for this unpalatable advice was the withholding of short-term aid by all Western governments should a given state fail to implement the IMF policy, and hence (given the debt crisis) the prospect of governmental insolvency. One African state after another would yield to the pressure, though none did as well as the only country that fully repaid a large debt in the 1980s, which was Ceaucescu's Romania, to the great joy of the IMF and the great anger of the Romanian people.

The "debt crisis" in Africa translated into much that was nasty: famines, unemployment, massive deterioration of infrastructure, civil wars, and the disintegration of state machineries. In southern Africa, the difficulties were compounded by the destabilization programs of the *apartheid* regime of South Africa fighting its rearguard action against the downward sweep of African liberation which was able to reach Johannesburg only in 1994. We will distort our understanding of Africa's serious plight of the 1980s, however, if we do not place it in the larger picture of the world-economy. The debt crisis of course occurred elsewhere as well, and indeed in terms of total sums involved most notably in Latin America. The debt crisis of the Third World (plus the socialist bloc) meant the end of lending these countries new money. Indeed, the flow of money in the 1980s was decidedly from South to North, and not in the other direction.

However, the problem of placing surplus-value profitably did not disappear, since the absence of sufficient lucrative outlets for productive investment continued. The collapse of the borrowers of the 1970s (including the African states) was no doubt a problem for these borrowers, but it was also a serious problem for the lenders, who needed to lend money to someone. In the 1980s they found two important new borrowers, and not minor ones: the major corporate enterprises of the world, and the government of the United States.

The 1980s is an era that will be remembered in the world of corporations as the era of junk bonds and of corporate takeovers. What was going on? Essentially, a lot of money was being invested in buying corporations, largely in order to chop them up, then sell off profitable chunks, and allow the other parts to rust away (in the process, laying off the workers). The outcome was not at all increased production but rather enormous debts for such corporations. As a result, many industrial corporations and banks went bankrupt. If they were big enough, as bankruptcy approached, the states intervened to "save" them because of the negative political and economic consequences. The result, as in the case of the savings-and-loan associations scandal in the U.S., was huge profits to the junk-bond dealers and a huge bill for the U.S. taxpayer.

The huge bill deriving from corporate debts was compounded, in the case of the U.S., by the huge debt of military Keynesianism. The Reagan non-revolution meant first of all, contrary to its own very loud rhetoric, a vast expansion of state involvement in the U.S. economy and in the size of its bureaucracy. Economically, what Reagan did was to reduce federal tax levels for the wealthier segments of the population (which resulted in further internal polarization) while simultaneously increasing massively military expenditures (which held back unemployment ratios). But as the 1980s went on, the U.S. borrowing was causing the same problems for it, as the Third World debt had caused for the Third World. There was however one difference. The IMF was in no position to impose IMF policies on the U.S., and politically the U.S. was unwilling to impose them on itself. But in the process, the U.S. economic position vis-à-vis its now strong competitors (western Europe and Japan) was constantly deteriorating precisely because of the military focus of U.S. investment.

It is at this point that the so-called collapse of the Communisms intervened. We have already noted that its accepted starting-point, the rise of Solidarność, in Poland was a direct outcome of the debt crisis. Essentially, the socialist countries faced the same negative consequences of the world economic stagnation as did the African states: end of the impressive growth rates of the A-period; decline in real standards of living, if not in the 1970s, then in the 1980s; deterioration of infrastructure; decline of governmental services; and above all, disillusionment with the regimes in power. The disillusionment focused on political repression but its motor was the failure of the promise of "development."

In the case of the U.S.S.R., the general problem of all the socialist states was compounded by the contradiction of the Yalta accord. The Yalta accord was, we have argued, a quite precise arrangement. It allowed for rhetorical struggle about the distant future but presumed a deal about the present, a deal that was sedulously respected. To do this, both sides had to be strong, strong enough to control all their satellites and allies. The ability of the U.S.S.R. to do its part was now compromised by the economic difficulties of the 1980s as well as, of course, by the deterioration of ideological coherence that started in 1956 with the XXth Party Congress. Its problems were made worse by the military Keynesianism of the U.S. which increased pressure on the U.S.S.R. to expend funds it did not have. However, the biggest dilemma of all was not U.S. military strength but the growing U.S. economic and political *weaknesses*. The U.S.-U.S.S.R. relationship was held together in the manner of a taut rubber band. If the U.S. weakened its hold, the link was untenable. The result was Gorbachev's desperate attempt to save the situation by forcing an end to the Cold War, disengaging from eastern Europe, and relaunching the U.S.S.R. internally. It turned out not to be possible, at least the third part, and the U.S.S.R. is no more.

The collapse of the U.S.S.R. has created enormous difficulties, perhaps insurmountable ones, for the U.S. It has eliminated the only political control the U.S. had over its now quite strong economic rivals, western Europe and Japan. While it kept the U.S. debt from further increasing by ending military Keynesianism, it created as a consequence a massive problem of economic deployment with which the U.S. has not coped very well. And ideologically, the collapse of Marxism-Leninism has eliminated the last credence that state-managed reformism could bring about significant economic development of the peripheral and semi-peripheral zones of the capitalist world-economy. That is why I have argued elsewhere that the so-called collapse of the Communisms was really the collapse of liberalism as an ideology. But liberalism as the dominant ideology of the geo-culture (already undermined in 1968, and mortally wounded by the events of 1989) has been a political pillar of the world-system, having been the main instrument by which the "dangerous classes" (first the European working classes in the nineteenth century, then the popular classes of the Third World in the twentieth) have been "tamed." Without credence in the efficacy of national liberation dosed with Marxism-Leninism, the popular classes of the Third World have little reason to be patient, and they will cease to be so.

Finally, the economic consequences of the end of military Keynesianism has been very bad news for Japan and East Asia, whose expansion in the 1980s had been strongly fueled by the ability to lend money to the U.S. government as well as to participate in the now dormant process of corporate takeovers. Thus the East Asian miracle, still real insofar as it we look at it in terms relative to the U.S., is now in trouble in absolute terms.

These dramatic transformations of the late 1980s have been marked in Africa (as in Latin America and in eastern Europe) by the rise of two leitmotivs: the market and democratization. Before we can look at the future, we must spend a moment dissecting them. The popularity of the "market" as organizing mantra is the counterpart of the disillusion with the "state" as organizing mantra. The problem is that it conveys two quite different messages. For some, particularly younger elite elements, erstwhile bureaucrats and/or socialist politicians, it is the great cry of pre-1848 France, "Messieurs, enrichissez-vous!" And, as has been true for some 500 years now, it is always possible for some new group to become "nouveaux riches."

But, for most people, the turn to the "market" does not signify any change in objective at all. Over the past decade, people in Africa (and elsewhere) have turned to the "market" for exactly the same thing as they had previously turned to the "state." What they hope to get is that elusive pot of gold at the end of the rainbow, "development." By "development," of course, they really mean equality, living as well as, as comfortably as, people do in the North, probably in particular as people do in American movies. But this is a profound illusion. Neither the "state" nor the "market" will promote egalitarian "development" in a capitalist world-economy, whose guiding principle of the ceaseless accumulation of capital requires and generates ever-greater polarization of real income. Since most people are reasonably intelligent and reasonably aware, it will not take too long for whatever magic attaches to the "market" as medicine to dissipate, and leave a stunning hangover.

Is "democratization" and its annexed slogan of "human rights" very different? Well, yes and no. First of all, we have to be clear what it is we mean by "democratization." Since 1945, there has been virtually no state in which there has not been regular elections of the legislature, with near-universal suffrage. Such procedures we all recognize can be meaningless. We seem to mean something more. But what is this more? Elections in which two or more parties contest? Contest really and not nominally, contest with votes counted correctly and not fraudulently, contest fairly and not have the results annulled? If adding such requirements is what it takes to move us in the direction of "democratization," then I suppose we have been making a little progress. But in an era when the *New York Times* reveals that the governing party of Japan over the last 40-odd years, the Liberal Democratic Party, has been receiving regular subsidies from the C.I.A., we may be allowed to doubt if the formality of freely-contested elections suffices to permit us to talk of democratization.

The problem, as we know, is that democracy, like the market, has two quite different affective connotations. One goes with the market as locus of enrichment; the other goes with the objective of egalitarian development. The first meaning of "democracy" appeals to a small, albeit powerful, group. The second appeals to a much larger, but politically weaker group. The efforts to achieve democratization in recent years in such bellwether African situations as Togo, Nigeria, and Zaire have not been terribly encouraging. Perhaps, however, real democracy can only be possible with real development, and if development is an illusion in the present world-system, democratization may not be much better.

Am I then preaching a doctrine of hopelessness? Not at all! But before we can have useful hope, we must have lucid analysis. The world-system is in disarray. Africa is in disarray, but not really more so than the rest of the world-system. Africa has emerged from an era of perhaps exaggerated optimism into a mood of pessimism. Well, so has the world. From 1945 to the late 1960s, everything seemed to be getting better and better everywhere. From the late 1960s to the late 1980s things started to go sour in various ways almost everywhere, and people began at the very least to rethink their easy optimism. Today we are frightened, diffusely angry, unsure of our verities, and in "disarray." This is simply the reflection in collective consciousness of a deep crisis in our existing world-system in which the traditional mechanisms of resolving normal cyclical downturns are no longer working so well, in which the secular trends of the world-system have led the system "far from equilibrium." We are therefore approaching a "bifurcation" (to use the language of the new science) whose outcome is inherently indeterminate, which can push us in possible alternative directions that are quite different the ones from the others.

If one wants to face up to Africa's dilemmas, the first thing to see is how they are not special to Africa. Let me take four dilemmas that are frequently discussed about Africa, and try to put each in a wider context. The first is the collapse of the national liberation movements. In almost every country, a movement emerged during colonial times which incarnated the demand for autonomous control by Africans of their own destiny and led the political battle to achieve this goal. These movements were a nationally-integrating force, mobilizing the populations in the name of a better life and a more equal world. They were against divisive particularisms within the state, but in favor of the assertion of national and African culture within the world-system. They were modernizing and democratizing movements, and they purveyed hope.

Yesterday, these movements achieved their primary objective of national independence. Today, none of these movements has survived intact; most have not survived at all. The only real exception is the ANC of South Africa, and it has achieved its primary objective only in 1994. Wherever these movements have crumbled in the post-independence era, no other political force has filled the vacuum or has been able to mobilize national consciousness in similar ways, nor are any such forces in sight.

This may be dismaying, but is this so special to Africa? Have national liberation movements fared better in South and Southeast Asia, in the Arab world, in Latin America and the Caribbean? Certainly the Communist movements that took power in a geographic stretch from the Elbe to the Yalu seem not to have fared any better. And if we look at western Europe, and the extra-European world of White settlement, is the picture really different? The movements there comparable to the national liberation movements of Africa are the Social-Democratic movements (*lato sensu*) who also mobilized popular opinion in modernizing, democratizing directions, and also in most cases were able after long decades of struggle to come to power. But are not these movements now also in "disarray," renouncing old slogans, unsure of what they stand for, and incapable of obtaining the kind of mass affective support which had been their force? Personally, I do not see much difference.

The second problem of which one talks derives in part from the collapse of these movements. What we mean by their collapse is the withdrawal of mass support. They can no longer mobilize anyone. But what about the mobilizers, the cadres of all these movements, the strata whose upward mobility had been made possible by the success of these movements—the politicians, the bureaucrats, the intellectuals? It was they who propagated the national project and in many ways it was they who profited most by it.

As the movements began to collapse, as the objectives for which the movements struggle seemed to recede into the horizon, these cadres seemed to scramble to shore, seeking individual salvation. The ideological commitments faded into the background, the selflessness of the period of nationalist struggle was abandoned, and many entered into a competitive scramble in which the line between the legitimate and the illegitimate became difficult to distinguish.

This is no doubt true of Africa of the 1990s. But is venal corruption of cynical elites an African specialty? I doubt it. We see the same phenomenon at work in Latin America and Asia. It is graphic in the ex-Communist world. And one needs only to read the headlines to realize that the corruption in Africa pales before that which daily comes to light in Italy and Japan, in France and the United States. Nor is this new, of course.

What created the disarray is not the corruption in high places, but the fact that, of all those who have benefited from the worldwide expansion of the "middle strata" in the period 1945-1970, so large a percentage of them have fallen off the Ferris wheel on its downward turn in the post-1970 period. This group that rose socially and economically, and then fell (whilst others had not fallen) are an acutely destabilizing force politically, harboring deep resentments, and turning to all kinds of anti-state, moralistic and moralizing movements to secure their personal safety and express their aggressions. But here too, Africa is not special. If anything, this problem is far more serious in Europe and North America than it is in Africa.

The third problem with which Africa is said to be faced is the disintegration of the state structures. Certainly Liberia or Somalia present extreme examples of this phenomenon. But once again we need to go beyond the glaring examples to look at the problem. The withdrawal of legitimation of the states resulting from the collapse of the national liberation movements is a first part of the problem. The new anti-state disposition of erstwhile cadres threatened with downward mobility is another part. But the most fundamental problem is the structural inability to provide egalitarian development, while the demand for democratization is ceaselessly growing. We have already discussed the strain in state resources that world economic stagnation has caused. States have been increasingly unable to provide services even at the inadequate levels they previously supplied them. This started a circular process. States have found it more difficult to raise revenues. Their ability to ensure order has declined. As the ability to ensure order declined, people have turned to other structures to provide security and welfare, which in turn has further weakened the states.

But here too the only reason this is so visible in Africa is that this decline in stateness has set in so soon after the states themselves were established. If we look at this worldwide, we can notice that there has been a secular trend of strengthening state structures over 500 years which seems to have reached its peak in the late 1960s and has started moving in the other direction everywhere. In the North, it gets discussed under various rubrics: the fiscal crisis of the states; the rise of urban crime and the creation of self-defense structures; the inability of the states to contain the influx of persons; the pressure to dismantle welfare state structures.

Finally, in Africa, many point to the collapse of physical infrastructure and the dangerous trends in epidemiology. This is of course true. Highway systems, educational systems, hospitals are in bad shape and getting worse, and the money to rectify the situation does not seem to be there. The spread of AIDS is proverbial. And even if its spread can be contained, there looms the dangers of new maladies spread by drug-resistant bacteria or viruses coming into existence.

Here again, the problem is dramatic in Africa but scarcely restricted to it. Just as we seem to have hit a peak in the strengthening of state structures some 25 years ago, we may also have hit a peak in the two-century-long worldwide attack on infectious and contagious diseases. The self-confident utilization of dramatic solutions may have undone some protective ecological mechanisms, making possible new kinds of terrible, previously unknown, epidemic diseases. The breakdown in physical infrastructure cannot help in this regard. In any case, at a time when new strains of tuberculosis are emerging in U.S. cities, it is hardly the moment to deem this an African problem.

If, however, the problem is not that of Africa but that of the world-system as a whole, is Africa destined merely to be a bystander in a world crisis, suffering its fate but not being able to do anything about it? My belief is quite the contrary. The crisis of the world-system is the opportunity of the world-system in general, and perhaps of Africa in particular. While we can expect in theory that the very processes of our present world-system will exacerbate and not eliminate the crisis, we know that this involves a disarray, a great world disorder over 25-50 years, out of which will come some new kinds or order.

What we all do in this transitional period in which we are living will determine whether the historical system(s) that will emerge at the end of this process will in fact be better or worse than the modern world-system though whose demise we find ourselves living. There is not merely room in this period for action at the local level. Action at the local level is the critical variable that will determine how we come out of the crisis.

There are no simple formulas. We need to analyze more clearly the existing world situation and divest our minds of categories and concepts that have closed our thinking to see the real historical alternatives that are or can become available. We need to organize and revitalize local solidarities that turn outward and not inward. Above all, we must become very clear that protection of our grouping that is in fact at the expense of some other grouping is self-destructive.

I think above all we need to keep our eye on the ball. A more equal distribution of goods, services, and power has got to be the basis on which we create our new historical system(s). Our time horizons have to be longer than they have been in terms of the use of our resources, natural and human. In this kind of reconstruction, Africa is well placed to take a lead. Africa has been a zone of exclusion in our modern world-system and we may expect that over the next 25-50 years the on-going political, economic, and cultural mechanisms of the world-system will operate to exclude Africa and Africans still more.

If Africans stay mired in the claim for inclusion within the world-system in its present definition, they will tilt at windmills. If Africans show the way of combining short-run local meliorations with middle-run transformation of values and structures, they will not only help Africa; they will help the rest of us as well. Do not ask me or other non-Africans to draw up a specific agenda for action. We cannot do it. The ball is very much in Africa's court.

Let me say one last thing. I do not say Africa will inevitably succeed, as it tries. Africa has, we all have, at best a 50-50 chance of coming out of this transition with something better. History is not necessarily on our side, and if we think it is, this belief will work against us. But we are all very much an important and integral part of this process. And if we engage in it in the right way, we may indeed achieve the kind of world-system we want. It is around this realization that the road is hard, the outcome uncertain, but the struggle worth it, that we must organize our collective efforts.

II

RISE OF IDENTITY POLITICS: WORLD-SYSTEM CONTEXT FOR AFRICAN DILEMMAS

5

THE CONSTRUCTION OF PEOPLEHOOD: RACISM, NATIONALISM, ETHNICITY[17]

Nothing seems more obvious than who or what is a people. Peoples have names, familiar names. They seem to have long histories. Yet any pollster knows that if one poses the open-ended question "what are you?" to individuals presumably belonging to the same "people," the responses will be incredibly varied, especially if the matter is not at that moment in the political limelight. And any student of the political scene knows that very passionate political debates hinge around these names. Are there Palestinians? Who is a Jew? Are Macedonians Bulgarians? Are Berbers Arabs? What is the correct label: Negro, Afro-American, Black (capitalized), black (uncapitalized)? People shoot each other every day over the question of labels. And yet, the very people who do so tend to deny that the issue is complex or puzzling or indeed anything but self-evident.

I would like to start by describing one recent debate about one particular people. It has the rare quality of being a relatively friendly debate, among people who assert they share common political objectives. It is a debate that was published in the explicit hope of resolving the issue amicably among comrades.

The setting is South Africa. The South African government has by law proclaimed the existence of four groups of "peoples," each with a name: Europeans, Indians, Coloureds, Bantus. Each of these legal categories is complicated and contains multiple possible subgroups within it. The sub-groups combined under one legal label are sometimes curious from the vantage point of an outsider. Nonetheless, these labels have the force of law and have very specific consequences for individuals. Each resident of South Africa is classified administratively into one of these four categories and as a result has different political and social rights. For example, he/she is required to live in a residential area assigned by the state to his category and in some cases to sub-categories.

There are a large number of people in South Africa opposed to this process of legal categorization, which is known as apartheid. The history of their opposition shows, however, at least one significant shift of tactics with regard to the legal labels. Originally, those opposed to apartheid formed organizations within the framework of each separate category. These organizations then formed a political alliance and worked together. For example, in 1955, there occurred a very famous Congress of the People, cosponsored by four groups, each composed of persons belonging to one of the government's four categories of peoples. This Congress of the People issued a Freedom Charter calling for, among other things, the end of apartheid.

The largest of the four opposition organizations was the African National Congress (ANC), which represented what the government called Bantus, some 80 percent of the total population falling under the state's jurisdiction. Somewhere in the 1960s or perhaps 1970s—it is not clear when—the ANC slipped into using the term "African" for all those who were not "Europeans" and thus included under the one label what the government called Bantus, Coloureds, and Indians. Some others—it is not clear who—made a similar decision but designated this group as "non-Whites" as opposed to "Whites." In any case, the consequence was to reduce a fourfold classification to a dichotomy.

The decision, if that is what it was, was not unambiguous, however. For example, the allied organization of the ANC among Indians, the South African Indian Congress (SAIC), continued to exist, though its president and others became simultaneously members of the SAIC and the ANC.

The category "Coloured" has no doubt been the most nettlesome of the four. This "group" was constituted historically out of descendants of various unions between African persons and European persons. It also included persons brought from the East Indies centuries ago, who came to be known as Cape Malays. The "Coloureds" were mostly persons who in other parts of the world have been called "mulattos" and who in the United States were always considered part of the "Negro race," in terms of the now-defunct laws governing racial segregation.

In June 1984, Alex La Guma, member of the ANC and a Coloured from the government's point of view, wrote a letter to the editor of *Sechaba*, the official journal of the ANC. He posed the following issue:

> I have noticed now in speeches, articles, interviews etc. in *Sechaba*, that I am called 'so-called Coloured' (sometimes with a small 'c'). When did the Congress decide to call me this? In South Africa I was active in the Congress Alliance and was a member of the Coloured People's Congress, not the 'so-called Coloured People's Congress.' When we worked for Congress of the People and the Freedom Charter we sang, 'We the Coloured people, we must struggle to exist....' I remember in those times some people of the so-called unity movement [a rival organization to the ANC] refer to so-called Coloured people, but not our Congress. The old copies of *Sechaba* do not show when it was decided to make this change, or why. Maybe governments, administrations, political and social dealings over centuries called me Coloured. But clever people, the ethnologists and professors of anthropology and so on did not bother to worry about who I really am.
>
> Comrade Editor, I am confused. I need clarification. It makes me feel like a 'so-called' human, like a humanoid, those things who have all the characteristics of human beings but are really artificial. Other minority people are not called 'so-called.' Why me? It must be the 'curse of Ham.'

There were three responses to this letter. The first, also in the June issue, was from the editor:

> As far as I can remember there is no decision taken in our movement to change from 'Coloured' to 'so-called Coloured.' All I know is that people at home—like Allan Boesak [Boesak is someone the government labels as Coloured] at the launch of the UDF [United Democratic Front, an anti-apartheid organization]—have been increasingly

using the term, 'so-called Coloureds.' I suspect that what you have noticed is a reflection of this development.

Not long ago, *Sechaba* reviewed Richard Rive's book, *Writing Black*, and in that review we said:

> Our strive for unity should not blind us from seeing the differences which if ignored can cause problems exactly for that unity we are striving to achieve. It is not enough to say the so-called Coloureds or to put the word Coloureds in inverted commas. A positive approach to this problem needs to be worked out because we are dealing with a group of people who are identifiable and distinguishable.

In other words, what we are saying in this review is that a discussion on this issue is necessary, and I think your letter may just as well be a starting point for such a discussion. Any comments on this issue are welcome.

In the August 1984 issue of *Sechaba*, there appeared a letter signed P. G. From the contents, it appears that P. G. is also someone labeled Coloured by the government. Unlike Alex La Guma, he rejects the term unequivocally.

> In the Western Cape, I can remember the discussion we used to have about the term Coloured, when we met as groups of the Comrades Movement. These were loosely organized groups of youth brought together in action and study through the uprising of 1976, and who were largely pro-ANC. The term, 'so-called Coloured,' was commonly used amongst the youth in popular expression of rejection of apartheid terminology.
>
> I am in full agreement with what was said in the *Sechaba* review of Richard Rive's *Writing Black*, but would add that while, as you say, 'It is not enough to say the 'so-called Coloureds' or to put the word Coloureds in inverted commas,' it would be equally wrong to accept the term, 'Coloured.' I say this especially in the light of the fact that most people are rejecting the term 'Coloured.' Congress people, UDF people, those in civic groups, church groups and trade unions, leaders popular with the people speak of 'so-called Coloured' without they, or the people they are speaking to, feeling like humanoids. In fact the use of the term 'Coloured' is cited as making people feel artificial. Coloured is a term which cries of lack of identity.
>
> The term 'Coloured' did not evolve out of a distinctive group, but was rather a label pinned on to a person whom the Population Registra-

tion Act of 1950 defines as 'who in appearance is obviously not White or Indian and who is not a member of an aboriginal race or African tribe.' A definition based on exclusion—that is, the isn't people.... The term 'Coloured' was given to what the racists viewed as the marginal people. The term 'Coloured' was fundamental to the racist myth of the pure white Afrikaner. To accept the term 'Coloured' is to allow the myth to carry on....

Today, people are saying, 'We reject the racists' framework, we reject their terminology,' and are beginning to build the NEW in defiance of the old, right in the midst of the enemy. The term 'Coloured-Kleurling,' like 'half-caste,' 'Bruine Afrikaner' and 'South Africa's step-children,' has been handed down by the racists. Instead of some of us getting offended or taken aback by adopting a very narrow interpretation of this usage, we should see the prefix 'so-called' as the first step in coming towards a solution of something which has been a scourge for years.

We have got to move on from the term 'so-called Coloured' in a positive way. People are now saying that we have the choice of what we will be called, and most, in the spirit of the nation in the making, opt for 'South African.' The debate can take many forms, but not a reverting to acceptance of the Baasskap term. If one really needs a sub-identity to that of being a South African, maybe through popular debate the question could be sorted out.

In the September 1984 issue of *Sechaba*, Arnold Selby, someone labeled by the government as a European, entered the debate utilizing a set of categories that distinguished between "nations" and "national minorities":

Let's start the ball rolling viewing some established and accepted facts:

(a) As yet there is no such thing as a South African nation;

(b) The African majority is an oppressed nation, the Coloured people and the Indian people are distinct identifiable oppressed national minorities, the White population comprises the minority oppressor nation;

(c) The Coloured, Indian and White national minorities are not homogeneous but embrace other national or ethnic groups. For example, the Lebanese community is in the main classified and regards itself as White, the Malay and Griqua people regard themselves as part of the Coloured nation, the Chinese minority finds some of its number classified as White, others as Asian and others as Coloured;

(d) The key to South Africa's future and the solution of the national question lies in the national liberation of the African nation. The victory of our national democratic revolution, headed by the African National Congress bringing with it the national liberation of the African nation, will set in motion the process for the birth of a South African nation.

As stated in (b) above, the Coloured people comprise a distinct identifiable oppressed national minority. But the definition, 'Coloured,' the terminology arising therefrom and its usage in the practice of daily life did not emerge from the natural social causes, nor were they chosen by the Coloured people. They were imposed upon the Coloured people by the successive regimes which came in the wake of successive waves of aggressions, penetration and settlement of South Africa by the European bourgeois nations, in both their trading and imperialist phases, and after the founding of the aggressor South African state in 1910....

Now let me come to the tendency on the part of some of us to talk about the 'so-called' Coloured people. This, I believe, arises from two real factors with which we are faced.

First is the question of our work abroad. Other countries and nations have different conceptions about the term 'Coloured people,' which are far out of keeping with the reality of the nationally oppressed Coloured national minority in our country. When we speak about our country and its struggle and the role and place of the Coloured people in this struggle we have to explain who the Coloured people are, hence we often find ourselves using the words 'so-called' (please note inverted commas) to emphasize the aggressors' imposition of the term. Like one could say the 'so-called' Indians when referring to the original inhabitants of what is now the USA. This gives a clearer picture to those abroad who want to know more about our liberation struggle.

Secondly, I do not believe that the tendency of some at home to use the words 'so-called' means a rejection of our generally accepted term 'Coloured people.' To my way of thinking the words are used to stress the growing unity of the oppressed Coloured and Indian national minorities with the oppressed majority African nation. The usage of these words, I believe, indicates an identification with Black rather than Coloured separation from Black. At the same time the usage distances the Coloured people from the White oppressor minority nation. Time without number the oppressor White minority nation has sought without success to get acceptance of the idea that the Coloured people are an inferior off-shoot of the White nation, to which it is naturally allied. The usage of 'so-called' means a rejection of the aggressor's attempts to get acceptance of such racist ideology clothed in scientific terminology.

> Whether we use 'so-called' or not, the reality is that there is an oppressed Coloured national minority in our country. In my opinion, under today's conditions, it is not incorrect to use 'so-called' provided it is done in the proper context to convey the true meaning and is put in inverted commas. Under no circumstances can there be a rejection of the reality of the existence of the Coloured people as an oppressed minority nation.

Note that Selby's position is really quite different from P. G.'s. While both accept the use of 'so-called' before 'Coloured,' P. G. does it because there is no such thing as Coloureds. Selby thinks Coloureds exist as a people, of a variety of people he calls 'national minorities,' but defends the use of 'so-called' as a tactic in political communication.

Finally, in the November 1984 issue, La Guma responds, unrepentant:

> [PG] says that 'so-called Coloured' was used in popular expression of rejection of 'apartheid terminology.' Yet later he says that 'most, in the spirit of a nation in the making, opt for 'South African.' 'But, Comrade Editor, he does not tell us who gave our country the official name of South Africa? On what or whose authority? There are some who, rejecting this 'terminology,' call the country 'Azania' (again, on whose authority?) and maybe they would call the rest of the population 'so-called South Africans.' But it would seem that even though the Boer anthem refers to Suid-Afrika, the name of South Africa is accepted. Yet for any minority (even so-called) to assume the right to call themselves South African for their own studied convenience seems to me to be somewhat undemocratic, if not downright presumptuous, since the right naturally belongs to the majority.
>
> I regret to say that I did not know (as PG seems to say) that the term 'Coloured' emerged as a result of the definition laid down by the Population Registration Act or the Group Areas Act. I was born long before these Acts, so our people must be a little older than that. And we should not believe that all the awful experiences described by PG (divided families, rejection, etc.) are only suffered by us. Mixed race or marginal communities in other parts of the world suffer similar trials and tribulations.
>
> Now PG even says 'so-called' is not good enough, but neither is 'Coloured,' which adds to my confusion, Comrade Editor. But it is not being called Coloured that has been 'a scourge for years,' but the way our people have been and are being treated, whatever they are called, just as the term 'Asiatic' or 'Indian' in itself does not mean

> scourged.... While I wait patiently for the outcome of PG's 'mass debate,' I would still like to know what I am today. So, Comrade Editor, call me what the devil you like, but for God's sake don't call me 'so-called.'

I have cited this exchange at some length to show first of all that even the most amicable of debates is quite passionate; and secondly, to show how difficult the issue is to resolve on either historical or logical grounds. Is there a Coloured people, or a Coloured national minority, or a Coloured ethnic group? Was there ever? I can say that some people think there is and/or was, others do not, still others are indifferent, and still others are ignorant of the category.

Ergo, what? If there is some essential phenomenon, a Coloured people, we should be able to come to terms about its parameters. But if we find that we cannot come to terms about this name designating a "people" or indeed about virtually any other name designating some people, maybe this is because peoplehood is not merely a construct but one which, in each particular instance, has constantly changing boundaries. Maybe a people is something that is supposed to be inconstant in form. But if so, why the passion? Maybe because no one is supposed to observe upon the inconstancy. If I am right, then we have a very curious phenomenon indeed—one whose central features are the reality of inconstancy and the denial of this reality. Very complicated, indeed bizarre, I should say! What is there in the historical system in which we are located that would give rise to such a curious social process? Perhaps there is a quark to locate.

I propose to address this issue in successive steps. Let us first review briefly the existing views in social science about peoplehood. Let us then see what there is in the structure and processes of this historical system that might have produced such a concept. Finally, let us see if there is some conceptual reformulation that might be useful.

To start with the literature of the historical social sciences, one must note that the term "people" is actually used somewhat infrequently. Rather the three commonest terms are "race," "nation," and "ethnic group," all presumably varieties of "peoples" in the modern world. The last of these three is the most recent and has replaced in effect the previously widely-used term of "minority." Of course, each of these terms has many variants, but nonetheless I think both statistically and logically these are the three modal terms.

A "race" is supposed to be a genetic category, which has a visible physical form. There has been a great deal of scholarly debate over the past 150 years as to the names and characteristics of races. This debate is quite famous and, for much of it, infamous. A "nation" is supposed to be a socio-political category, linked somehow to the actual or potential boundaries of a state. An "ethnic group" is supposed to be a cultural category, of which there are said to be certain continuing behaviors that are passed on from generation to generation and that are not normally linked in theory to state boundaries.

The three terms are used with incredible inconsistency, of course, leaving quite aside the multitude of other terms utilized. (We have already seen, in the above debate, one person designates as a "national minority" what others might have called an "ethnic group.") Most users of the terms use them, all three of them, to indicate some persisting phenomenon which, by virtue of its continuity, not only has a strong impact on current behavior but also offers a basis for making present-day political claims. That is, a "people" is said to be or act as it does because of either its genetic characteristics, or its socio-political history, or its "traditional" norms and values.

The whole point of these categories seems to be to enable us to make claims based upon the past against the manipulable "rational" processes of the present. We may use these categories to explain why things are the way they are and shouldn't be changed, or why things are the way they are and can't be changed. Or conversely we may use them to explain why the present structures should indeed be superseded in the name of deeper and more ancient, ergo more legitimate, social realities. The temporal dimension of pastness is central to and inherent in the concept of peoplehood.

Why does one want or need a past, an "identity?" This is a perfectly sensible question to ask and is even on occasion asked. Notice, for example, that P. G. in the cited debate advocates discarding the appellation "Coloured" in favor of a larger category "South African" and then says: "If one really needs a sub-identity to that of being a South African...." If... implies why.

Pastness is a mode by which persons are persuaded to act in the present in ways they might not otherwise act. Pastness is a tool persons use against each other. Pastness is a central element in the socialization of individuals, in the maintenance of group solidarity, in the establishment of or challenge to social legitimation. Pastness therefore is preeminently a moral phenomenon, therefore a political phenomenon, always a contemporary phenomenon. That is of course why it is so inconstant. Since the real world is constantly changing, what is relevant to contemporary politics is necessarily constantly changing. Ergo, the content of pastness necessarily constantly changes. Since, however, pastness is by definition an assertion of the constant past, no one can ever admit that any particular past has ever changed or could possibly change. The past is normally considered to be inscribed in stone and irreversible. The real past, to be sure, is indeed inscribed in stone. The social past, how we understand this real past, on the other hand, is inscribed at best in soft clay.

This being the case, it makes little difference whether we define pastness in terms of genetically continuous groups (races), historical socio-political groups (nations), or cultural groups (ethnic groups). They are all peoplehood constructs, all inventions of pastness, all contemporary political phenomena. If this is so, however, we then have another analytic puzzle. Why should three different modal terms have developed when one term might have served? There must be some reason for the separation of one logical category into three social categories. We have but to look at the historical structure of the capitalist world-economy to find it.

Each of the three modal terms hinges around one of the basic structural features of the capitalist world-economy. The concept of "race" is related to the axial division of labor in the world-economy, the core-periphery antinomy. The concept of "nation" is related to the political superstructure of this historical system, the sovereign states that form and derive from the interstate system. The concept of "ethnic group" is related to the creation of household structures that permit the maintenance of large components of non-waged labor in the accumulation of capital. None of the three terms is directly related to class. That is because "class" and "peoplehood" are orthogonally defined, which as we shall see is one of the contradictions of this historical system.

The axial division of labor within the world-economy has engendered a spatial division of labor. We speak of a core-periphery antinomy as constitutive of this division of labor. Core and periphery strictly speaking are relational concepts that have to do with differential cost structures of production. The location of these different production processes in spatially-distant zones is not an inevitable and constant feature of the relationship. But it tends to be a normal one. There are several reasons for this. To the extent that peripheral processes are associated with primary production—which has in fact been historically true, although far less today than previously—then there is constraint on the geographical relocatability of these processes, associated with environmental conditions for cultivation or with geological deposits. Secondly, insofar as there are political elements in maintaining a set of core-peripheral relationships, the fact that products in a commodity chain cross political frontiers facilitates the necessary political processes, since the control of frontier transit is among the greatest real powers the states actually exercise. Thirdly, the concentration of core processes in states different from those in which peripheral processes are concentrated tends to create differing internal political structures in each, a difference which in turn becomes a major sustaining bulwark of the inegalitarian interstate system that manages and maintains the axial division of labor.

Hence, to put the matter simply, we tend over time to arrive at a situation in which some zones of the world are largely the loci of core production processes and others are largely the loci of peripheral production processes. Indeed, although there are cyclical fluctuations in the degree of polarization, there is a secular trend towards a widening of this gap. This world-wide spatial differentiation took the political form primarily of the expansion of a Europe-centered capitalist world-economy into one that eventually covered the globe. This came to be known as the phenomenon of the "expansion of Europe."

In the evolution of the human species on the planet Earth, there occurred in a period preceding the development of settled agriculture, a distribution of genetic variants such that at the outset of the development of the capitalist world-economy, different genetic types in any one location were considerably more homogeneous than they are today.

As the capitalist world-economy expanded from its initial location primarily in Europe, as concentrations of core and peripheral production processes became more and more geographically disparate, "racial" categories began to crystallize around certain labels. It may be obvious that there are a large series of genetic traits that vary, and vary considerably, among different persons. It is not at all obvious that these have to be coded as falling into three, five, or fifteen reified groupings we call "races." The number of categories, indeed the fact of any categorization, is a social decision. What we observe is that, as the polarization increased, the number of categories became fewer and fewer. When W. E. B. Du Bois said in 1900 that "the problem of the twentieth century is the problem of the color line," the colors to which he was referring came down in reality to white and non-white.

Race, and therefore racism, is the expression, the promoter, and the consequence of the geographical concentrations associated with the axial division of labor. That this is so has been made stunningly clear by the decision of the South African state in the last twenty years to designate visiting Japanese businessmen not as Asians (which local Chinese are considered to be) but rather as "honorary white." In a country whose laws are supposed to be based on the permanence of genetic categories, apparently genetics follows the election returns of the world-economy. Such absurd decisions are not limited to South Africa. South Africa merely got itself into the box of putting absurdities on paper.

Race is not, however, the only category of social identity we use. It apparently is not enough; we use nation as well. As we said, nation derives from the *political* structuring of the world-system. The states that are today members of the United Nations are all creations of the modern world-system. Most of them did not even exist either as names or as administrative units more than a century or two ago. For those very few that can trace a name and a continuous administrative entity in roughly the same geographical location to a period prior to 1450—there are fewer of these than we think: France, Russia, Portugal, Denmark, Sweden, Switzerland, Morocco, Japan, China, Iran, Ethiopia are perhaps the least ambiguous cases—it can still be argued that even these states came into existence as modern sovereign states only with the emergence of the present world-system. There are some other modern states that can trace a more discontinuous history of the use of a name to describe a zone—for example, Greece, India, Egypt. We get onto still thinner ice with such names as Turkey, Germany, Italy, Syria. The fact is that if we look forward from the vantage-point of 1450 at many entities that then existed—for example, the Burgundian Netherlands, the Holy Roman Empire, the Mughal Empire—we find we have today in each case not one state but at the very least three sovereign states that can argue some kind of political, cultural, spatial descent from these entities.

And does the fact that there are now three states mean that there are three nations? Is there a Belgian, a Dutch, a Luxemburg nation today? Most observers seem to think so. If there is, is this not because there came into existence *first* a Dutch state, a Belgian state, a Luxemburg state? A systematic look at the history of the modern world will show, I believe, that in almost every case statehood preceded nationhood, and not the other way around, despite a widespread myth to the contrary.

To be sure, once the interstate system was functioning, nationalist movements did arise in many zones demanding the creation of new sovereign states, and these movements sometimes achieved their objectives. But two caveats are in order. These movements, with rare exceptions, arose within already constructed administrative boundaries. Hence it could be said that a state, albeit a non-independent one, preceded the movement. And secondly, it is debatable how deep a root "nation" as a communal sentiment took before the actual creation of the state. Take for example the case of the Sahrawi people. Is there a Sahrawi nation? If you ask Polisario, the national liberation movement, they will say yes, and add that there has been one for a thousand years. If you ask the Moroccans, there never has been a Sahrawi nation, and the people who live in what was once the colony of the Spanish Sahara were always part of the Moroccan nation. How can we resolve this difference intellectually? The answer is that we cannot. If by the year 2000 or perhaps 2020, Polisario wins the current war, there will have been a Sahrawi nation. And if Morocco wins, there will not have been. Any historian writing in 2100 will take it as a settled question, or more probably still as a non-question.

Why should the establishment of any particular sovereign state within the interstate system create a corresponding "nation," a "people"? This is not really difficult to understand. The evidence is all around us. States in this system have problems of cohesion. Once recognized as sovereign, the states frequently find themselves subsequently threatened by both internal disintegration and external aggression. To the extent that "national" sentiment develops, these threats are lessened. The governments in power have an interest in promoting this sentiment, as do all sorts of sub-groups within the state. Any group who sees advantage in using the state's legal powers to advance its interests against groups outside the state or in any sub-region of the state has an interest in promoting nationalist sentiment as a legitimation of its claims. States furthermore have an interest in administrative uniformity that increases the efficacy of their policies. Nationalism is the expression, the promoter, and the consequence of such state-level uniformities.

There is another reason for the rise of nationalism, even more important. The interstate system is not a mere assemblage of so-called sovereign states. It is a hierarchical system with a pecking order that is stable but changeable. That is to say, slow shifts in rank order are not merely possible, but historically normal. Inequalities that are significant and firm but not immutable are precisely the kind of processes that lead to ideologies able to justify high rank but also to challenge low rank. Such ideologies we call nationalisms. For a state not to be a nation is for that state to be outside the game of either resisting or promoting the alteration of its rank. But then that state would not be part of the interstate system. Political entities that existed outside of and/or prior to the development of the interstate system as the political superstructure of a capitalist world-economy did not need to be "nations," and were not. Since we misleadingly use the same word, "state," to describe both these other political entities and the states created within the interstate system, we often miss the obvious inevitable link between the statehood of these latter "states" and their nationhood.

If we then ask what is served by having two categories—races and nations—instead of one, we see that while racial categorization arose primarily as a mode of expressing and sustaining the core-periphery antinomy, national categorization arose originally as a mode of expressing the competition between states in the slow but regular permutation of the hierarchical order and therefore of the detailed degree of advantage in the system as opposed to the cruder racial classification. In an oversimplified formula, we could say that race and racism unifies intra-zonally the core zones and the peripheral zones in their battles with each other, whereas nation and nationalism divides core zones and peripheral zones intra-zonally in the more complex intra-zonal as well as inter-zonal competition for detailed rank order. Both categories are claims to the right to possess advantage in the capitalist world-economy.

If all this were not enough, we have created the category of the ethnic group, the erstwhile minority. For there to be minorities, there needs to be a majority. It has long been noticed by analysts that minorityhood is not necessarily an arithmetically-based concept; it refers to the degree of social power. Numerical majorities can be social minorities. The location within which we are measuring this social power is not of course the world-system as a whole, but the separate states. The concept "ethnic group" is therefore as linked in practice to state boundaries as is the concept "nation," despite the fact that this is never included in the definition. The difference is only that a state tends to have *one* nation and *many* ethnic groups.

The capitalist system is based not merely on the capital-labor antinomy that is permanent and fundamental to it but on a complex hierarchy within the labor segment in which, although all labor is exploited because it creates surplus-value that is transferred to others, some laborers "lose" a larger proportion of their created surplus-value than others. The key institution that permits this is the household of part-lifetime wage laborers. These households are constructed in such a way that these wage workers may receive less in hourly wages than what is, on a proportionate calculation, the cost of the reproduction of labor. This is a very widespread institution, covering the majority of the world's workforce. I shall not repeat here the arguments for this analysis which have been made elsewhere.[18] I merely wish to discuss its consequences in terms of peoplehood. Wherever we find wage workers located in different kinds of household structures, from more highly-paid workers located in more "proletarianized" household structures to less highly-paid ones located in more "semi-proletarianized" household structures, we tend to find at the same time that these varieties of household structures are located inside "communities" called "ethnic groups." That is, along with an occupational hierarchy comes the "ethnicization" of the workforce within a given state's boundaries. Even without a comprehensive legal framework to enforce this, as in South Africa today, or the United States yesterday, there has been a very high correlation everywhere of ethnicity and occupation, provided one groups "occupations" into broad and not narrow categories.

There seem to be various advantages to the ethnicization of occupational categories. Different kinds of relations of production, we may assume, require different kinds of normal behavior by the workforce. Since this behavior is not in fact genetically determined, it must be taught. Work forces need to be socialized into reasonably specific sets of attitudes. The "culture" of an ethnic group is precisely the set of rules into which parents belonging to that ethnic group are pressured to socialize their children. The state or the school system can do this of course. But they usually seek to avoid performing that particularistic function alone or too overtly, since it violates the concept of "national" equality for them to do so. Those few states willing to avow such a violation are under constant pressure to renounce the violation. But "ethnic groups" not only *may* socialize their respective members differently from each other; it is the very definition of an ethnic group that they socialize in a particular manner. Thus what is illegitimate for the state to do comes in by the rear window as "voluntary" group behavior defending a social "identity."

This therefore provides a legitimation to the hierarchical reality of capitalism that does not offend the formal equality before the law which is one of its avowed political premises. The quark for which we were looking may be there. Ethnicization, or peoplehood, resolves one of the basic contradictions of historical capitalism—its simultaneous thrust for theoretical equality and practical inequality—and it does so by utilizing the mentalities of the world's working strata.

In this effort, the very inconstancy of peoplehood categories of which we have been speaking turns out to be crucially important. For while capitalism as an historical system requires constant inequality, it also requires constant restructuring of economic processes. Hence what guarantees a particular set of hierarchical social relations today may not work tomorrow. The behavior of the work-force must change without undermining the legitimacy of the system. The recurrent birth, restructuring, and disappearance of ethnic groups is thereby an invaluable instrument of flexibility in the operation of the economic machinery.

Peoplehood is a major institutional construct of historical capitalism. It is an essential pillar, and as such has grown more and more important as the system has developed greater density. In this sense it is like sovereign statehood, which is also an essential pillar, and has also grown more and more important. We are growing more, not less, attached to these basic *Gemeinschaften* formed within our world-historical *Gesellschaft*, the capitalist world-economy.

Classes are really quite a different construct from peoples, as both Marx and Weber knew well. Classes are "objective" categories, that is, analytic categories, statements about contradictions in an historical system, and not descriptions of social communities. The issue is whether and under what circumstances a class community can be created. This is the famous *an sich/für sich* distinction. Classes *für sich* have been a very elusive entity.

Perhaps, and here is where we will end, the reason is that the constructed "peoples"—the races, the nations, the ethnic groups—correlate so heavily, albeit imperfectly, with "objective class." The consequence has been that a very high proportion of class-based political activity in the modern world has taken the form of people-based political activity. The percentage will turn out to be even higher than we usually think if we look closely at so-called "pure" workers' organizations that quite frequently have had implicit and *de facto* "people" bases, even while utilizing a non-people, purely class terminology.

For more than a hundred years, the world left has bemoaned its dilemma that the world's workers have all too often organized themselves in "people" forms. But this is not a soluble dilemma. It derives from the contradictions of the system. There cannot be *für sich* class activity that is entirely divorced from people-based political activity. We see this in the so-called national liberation movements, in all the new social movements, in the anti-bureaucratic movements in socialist countries.

Would it not make more sense to try to understand peoplehood for what it is—in no sense a primordial stable social reality, but a complex, clay-like historical product of the capitalist world-economy through which the antagonistic forces struggle with each other. We can never do away with peoplehood in this system nor relegate it to a minor role. On the other hand, we must not be bemused by the virtues ascribed to it, or we shall be betrayed by the ways in which it legitimates the existing system. What we need to analyze more closely are the possible directions in which, as peoplehood becomes ever more central to this historical system, it will push us, at the system's bifurcation point, towards various possible alternative outcomes in the uncertain process of the transition from our present historical system to the one or ones that will replace it.

6

AFTER DEVELOPMENTALISM AND GLOBALIZATION, WHAT?[19]

In 1900, in preparation for the Exposition Universelle in Paris, the French Ministry of Colonies asked Camille Guy, the head of its geographical service, to produce a book entitled *Les colonies françaises: la mise en valeur de notre domaine coloniale*.[20] A literal translation of *mise en valeur* is "making into value." The dictionary, however, translates "mise en valeur" as "development." At the time, this expression was preferred, when talking about economic phenomena in the colonies, to the perfectly acceptable French word, "*développement*." If one then goes to *Les Usuels de Robert: Dictionnaire des Expressions et Locutions figurées* (1979) to learn more about the meaning of the expression "mettre en valeur," one finds the explanation that it is used as a metaphor meaning "to exploit, draw profit from."

Basically, this was the view of the pan-European world during the colonial era concerning economic development in the rest of the world. Development was a set of concrete actions effectuated by Europeans to exploit and draw profit from the resources of the non-European world. There were a number of assumptions in this view: Non-Europeans would not be able or perhaps even willing to "develop" their resources without the active intrusion of the pan-European world. But such development represented a material and moral good for the world. It was therefore the moral and political duty of the pan-Europeans to exploit the resources of these countries. There was consequently nothing wrong with the fact that, as a reward, the pan-Europeans who exploited the resources drew profit from them, since a secondary advantage would go to the persons whose resources were being exploited in this way.

This rationale of course completely omitted discussion of the cost in life and limb to the local people of such exploitation. The conventional calculus was that these costs were, as we would say in today's euphemisms, the necessary and inevitable "collateral damage" of Europe's "civilizing mission."

The tone of the discussion began to change after 1945, primarily as a result of the strength of anti-colonial sentiments and movements in Asia and Africa, and a new sense of collective assertiveness in Latin America. It is at this point that "development" came to be used as a code word for the belief that it was possible for the countries of the South to "develop" *themselves*, as opposed to "being developed" by the North. The new assumption was that, if the countries of the South would only adopt the proper policies, they would one day, some time in the future, become as technologically modern and as wealthy as the countries of the North.

At some point in the post-1945 period, Latin American authors began to call this new ideology "*desarollismo*" or "developmentalism." The ideology of developmentalism took a number of different forms. The Soviet Union called it instituting "socialism," which became defined as the last stage before "communism." The United States called it "economic development." Ideologues in the South often used the two terms interchangeably. Amidst this worldwide consensus, all the states of the North—the United States, the Soviet Union (and its East European satellites), the West European colonial (now becoming ex-colonial) powers, and the Nordic countries plus Canada—began to offer "aid" and advice concerning this development that everyone favored. The Economic Commission for Latin America (CEPAL) developed a new language of "core-periphery" relations, used primarily to justify a program of "import-substitution industrialization." And more radical Latin American (and other) intellectuals developed a language about "dependency," which, they said, needed to be fought against and overcome in order that dependent countries be in a position to develop.

The terminology may have differed but the one thing that was agreed upon by everyone was that development was indeed possible, if only.... When therefore the United Nations declared that the 1970s would be the "decade of development," the term and the objective seemed virtually a piety. Yet, as we know, the 1970s turned out to be a very bad decade for most of the countries of the South. It was the decade of the two successive oil price increases instituted by OPEC and of stagflation in the North. The consequent rise in the cost of imports for countries in the South combined with a sharp decline in the value of their exports because of the stagnation in the world-economy created acute balance of payments difficulties for just about every one of these countries (including those in the so-called socialist bloc), with the sole exception of those which were oil-exporting states.

The oil-exporting states acquired incredibly large surpluses, a large part of which they deposited in banks in the United States and Germany, who thereupon needed to find a remunerative use for this extra capital. They found it in loans to states with acute balance of payments difficulties. These loans, actively promoted by the banks themselves, solved both problems: finding an outlet for the surplus money in the accounts of the banks of the North and solving the liquidity problems of the virtually insolvent states of the South. But, alas, the loans led to cumulative interest payments which, by 1980, had led to even greater balance of payments difficulties in these states. Loans unfortunately are supposed to be repaid. The world thus arrived at the suddenly discovered so-called debt crisis—Poland in 1980, Mexico in 1982, and then all over the place.

It was easy enough to find the villain in the piece. The finger was pointed at developmentalism, so universally praised just a decade before. Import-substitution industrialization was now perceived as corrupt protectionism. State-building was deconstructed as feeding a bloated bureaucracy. Financial aid was now analyzed as money poured down a sink, if not a gutter. And parastatal structures, far from being virtuous efforts at pulling oneself up by one's own bootstraps, were exposed as deadening barriers to fruitful entrepreneurial achievement. It was decided that loans to states in distress, to be beneficial, needed to be hedged by requirements that these states cut wasteful state expenditures on such deferrable items as schools and health. It was further proclaimed that state enterprises were almost by definition inefficient, and should be privatized as rapidly as possible, since private enterprises were again almost by definition responsive to the "market" and therefore maximally efficient. Or at least that was the Consensus in Washington.

Academic buzz words and fads are fickle and usually last but a decade or two. Development was suddenly out. Globalization arrived in its wake. University professors, foundation executives, book publishers, and op-ed columnists all saw the light. To be sure, the optic, or better said the remedies, had changed. Now, the way to move forward was not to import-substitute but to export-orient productive activities. Down not only with nationalized industries but with capital transfer controls; up with transparent, unhindered flows of capital. In place of one-party regimes, let us all together study governance (a new word, splendidly erudite and quite inscrutable, if not meaningless). Above all, let us face Mecca five times a day and intone Allahu Akbar TINA—There is No Alternative.

The new dogmas took root in the 1980s amidst the decaying rot of develop mentalist dreams. They flourished in the 1990s bathed by the sparkle of the "new economy" in which the United States and eastern Asia were supposed to be leading the world to its economic glory. But alas, the sheen began to tarnish. The currency crisis in East and Southeast Asia in 1997 (which spread to Russia and Brazil), the slide downward of the World Trade Organization from Seattle to Cancun, the fading of Davos and the spectacular rise of Porto Alegre, al-Qaeda and September 11, followed by the Bush fiasco in Iraq and the current accounts crisis of the United States—all this and more leads one to suspect that globalization as rhetoric may be going quickly the way of developmentalism. And hence our question—After Developmentalism and Globalization, What?

Let us not be too acerbic about faded theorizing. The whole discussion from 1945 to today has indeed been one long effort to take seriously the reality that the world-system is not only polarized but polarizing, and that this reality is both morally and politically intolerable. For the countries at the bottom, there seemed nothing more urgent than figuring out how to improve their situation, and first of all economically. After all, all these people had to do was see a movie and they would know that there were other people and places in the world that were better off, far better off, than they were. As for the countries at the top, they realized, however dimly, that the "huddled masses yearning to breathe free" represented a permanent danger to world order and their own prosperity, and that therefore something, somehow had to be done to dampen the tinderbox.

So, the intellectual analyses and the derived policy efforts represented by the discussion about development and globalization were serious and respectable, if in retrospect quite misguided in many ways. The first question we need to ask now is, is it at all possible for every part of the world to attain—one day in a plausibly not too remote future—the standard of living of say Denmark (and perhaps also similar political and cultural institutions)? The second question is, if it is not, is it possible for the present lopsided and highly inegalitarian world-system to persist, more or less as such? And the third question is, if it is not, what kinds of alternatives present themselves to all of us now?

I

"Is it at all possible for every part of the world to attain - one day in a plausibly not too remote future - the standard of living of say Denmark (and perhaps also similar political and cultural institutions)?"

There is no question that Denmark (and most OECD countries) have a quite decent standard of living for a substantial proportion of their population. The standard measure of internal variation of income, the Gini curve, shows quite low numbers for most OECD countries, and by world standards reasonably good ones for all of them.[21] To be sure, there are many poor people in these countries, but compared to almost any country of the South, far fewer. So, of course, people in these poorer countries aspire to be as rich as people in Denmark. In the last few years, the world economic press has been full of stories about the remarkable rates of growth of China—a country which not too long ago was considered to be one of the poorest—along with much speculation about whether or not and to what degree these rates of growth can continue in the future and thereby transform China into a relatively wealthy country in terms of GDP per capita.

Let us leave aside the fact that many, many other countries have shown remarkable growth spurts for as much as up to 20-30 years, which rates then nonetheless petered out. There are, for example, the recent cases of the Soviet Union and Yugoslavia. Let us also leave out of the equation the long list of countries whose GDP was better in the further past than in the present. Let us assume for a moment that China's economic growth continues unhindered for another twenty years, and that China's GDP per capita approaches, let us say, if not that of Denmark at least that of Portugal or even Italy. Let us even speculate that up to 50% of its population benefits significantly from this growth spurt, which is then reflected in their real income.

Is it credible to hold everything else constant, and to assume that, at the very least, everyone else remains where they are today in terms of standard of living? Where is the surplus-value to come from that would permit 50% of China's population to consume at the level of 50% of Italy's population, while all the rest of the world consumes at a level at least as high as at present? Is this all supposed to come from the so-called greater productivity of world (or Chinese) production? It is clear that the skilled workers of Ohio and the Ruhr valley do not think so. They think they would pay for it, that they are already paying for it, by significantly reduced standards of living. Are they really so wrong? Has this not been happening in the past decade?

The first piece of evidence is the entire past history of the capitalist world-economy. In over five hundred years of its existence, the gap between the top and the bottom, the core and the periphery, has never gotten smaller, always larger. What is there in the present situation that should lead us to assume that this pattern would not continue? Of course, over those five hundred years, there is no question that some countries have improved their relative standing in the distribution of wealth in the world-system. Thus, it could be claimed that these countries had "developed" in some sense. But it is also true that other countries are lower in relative wealth rankings than earlier, some of them spectacularly so. And, although our statistical data is at most of even minimal quality only for the last 75-100 years, such comparative studies as we have do show a constant trimodal distribution of wealth in the world-system, with a few countries moving from one category to another.[22]

The second piece of evidence is that high levels of profit, and therefore of the possibility of accumulating surplus-value, correlates directly with the relative degree of monopolization of productive activity.[23] What we have been calling development for the last fifty years or so is basically the ability of some countries to erect productive enterprises of a type considered to be highly profitable. To the extent that they succeed in doing this, they thereby reduce the degree of monopolization of production in this particular arena and hence reduce the degree of profitability of such production. The historic pattern of successive so-called leading industries—from textiles to steel and automobiles to electronics to computer technology—Is clear evidence of this. The U.S. pharmaceutical industry is right now fighting a rear-guard battle against just such decline in potential profitability. Can Boeing and Airbus maintain their present profit levels in the face of competition by a putative Chinese aircraft construction industry twenty or thirty years from now?

So, basically, of two things one. Either the rising, so-called newly-developing countries will be crushed by some highly destructive process—warfare, plague, or civil war. And in this case, the existing economic centers of accumulation will remain on top, and the polarization will be still more acute. Or the rising, newly-developing countries will be able to reproduce some of the major productive processes of the present centers. And in this case, either the polarization will simply be inverted (which is unlikely) or there will be a flattening of the curve, But in this latter case, the ability to accumulate surplus-value in the world-economy taken as a whole will diminish severely, and the *raison d'être* of a capitalist world-economy will be undermined. In none of these scenarios does every country become a Denmark.

If there has come to be a general morosity about economic development and the positive benefits of globalization, it is, I would argue, because the sense that we are in a cul-de-sac has begun to creep in on more and more people—scholars, politicians, and above all ordinary workers. The optimism of the 1950s and 1960s, which was momentarily revived in the 1990s, is no longer with us.

I personally can see no way in which, within the framework of a capitalist world-economy, we can approach a general equalization of the distribution of wealth in the world, and even less an equalization that would have everyone consume at the level of the modal Danish consumer. I say this, taking into account all possible technological advances as well as increases in that elusive concept, productivity.

11

"If it is not [possible for all countries to achieve a Danish standard of living within the framework of the world-system in which we live], is it possible for the present lopsided and highly inegalitarian world-system to persist, more or less as such?"

I doubt it. But of course we must be careful here, since predictions of dramatic structural change have been made so frequently over the past two centuries, and have turned out to be inaccurate over a medium term because some crucial elements were left out of the analyses.

The major explanation of purported prospective fundamental structural change has been dissatisfaction of the exploited and oppressed. As conditions worsened, the people at the bottom, or some very large group, were destined—it was argued—to rebel. There would be what has usually been called a revolution. I shall not resume the arguments and counterarguments, which are no doubt quite familiar to almost anyone who has been seriously studying the history of the modern world-system.

The twentieth century was, among other things, the moment of a long series of national uprisings and social movements which proclaimed their revolutionary intents and which achieved state power in one form or another. The high point of these movements was the period 1945-1970, the period precisely of the flourishing of developmentalism, which was in some sense the credo of these movements. But we also know that the period 1970-2000 saw the downfall of most of these movements in power, or at least a drastic revision in their policies. This was the period of the flourishing of globalization, whose logic these movements—those still in power or those now seeking to play a role of parliamentary opposition—sullenly accepted. So, we have the era of triumphalism followed by the era of disillusionment.

Some of the cadres of these movements adjusted to what were thought to be the new realities and others jumped ship, either into passive withdrawal or into joining actively the erstwhile enemy. In the 1980s and until the mid-1990s, antisystemic movements worldwide were in a bad way. By 1995, however, the momentary sheen of neoliberalism had begun to wear off and there ensued a worldwide search for new antisystemic strategies. The story from Chiapas to Seattle to Porto Alegre has been that of the emergence of a new kind of world antisystemic movement, sometimes called these days *altermondialisme*. My name for it is the spirit of Porto Alegre and I think it is going to be an important element in the world political struggles of the next 25-50 years. I shall return to it in my discussion of real alternatives now.

However, I do not believe that a new version of revolutionary movement is the fundamental factor in what I see as the structural collapse of the capitalist world-economy. Systems collapse not primarily because of rebellion from below but because of the weaknesses of the dominant classes and the impossibility of their maintaining their level of gain and privilege. It is only when the existing system is weakened in terms of its own logic that the push from below can possibly be effective.

The basic strength of capitalism as a system has been twofold. On the one hand, it has demonstrated an ability to ensure, against all odds, the endless accumulation of capital. And on the other hand, it has put into place political structures that have made it possible to guarantee this endless accumulation of capital without being dethroned by the rash and dissatisfied "dangerous classes." The basic weakness of capitalism as an historical system today is that success is leading to failure (as Schumpeter taught us normally happens). As a consequence, today, both the ability to guarantee the endless accumulation of capital and the political structures that have kept the dangerous classes in line are collapsing simultaneously.

The success of capitalism in ensuring the endless accumulation of capital has been in its ability to keep the three basic costs of production—costs of personnel, costs of inputs, and taxation—from escalating too fast. However, it has done this by mechanisms that have been exhausting themselves over historical time. The system has now begun to reach a point where these costs are dramatically too high to make production an adequate source of capital accumulation. The capitalist strata have turned to financial speculation as a substitute. Financial speculation, however, is intrinsically a transitory mechanism, since it is dependent on confidence, and confidence in the medium run is undermined by the very speculation itself. Allow me to illustrate each of these points.

The costs of personnel are a function of the ongoing, never-ending class struggle. What the workers have on their side is the concentration of production (for reasons of efficiency) and hence their ability over time to organize themselves in both the work place and the political arena to put pressures on the employers to increase their remuneration. To be sure, employers always fight back by playing one set of workers off against another. But there are limits to doing this within the framework of a single country or a single local area, since there are political means by which the workers can encrust their advantages (legally and/or culturally).

Whenever we are in a Kondratieff A-phase, employers, faced with militant worker demands, usually prefer to allow remuneration to rise somewhat, since work stoppages do them more immediate damage than concessions. But as soon as we are in a Kondratieff B-phase, it becomes imperative for an employer who hopes to survive the bad times to reduce the remuneration package, since there is acute price competition. It is at this point that employers have historically resorted to relocation—the "runaway factory"—transferring their production to zones that have "historically"-lower rates of remuneration. But exactly what history accounts for these historically-lower rates? The answer is rather simple—the existence of a large pool of rural labor, for whom urban, waged employment, at whatever level of remuneration, represents a net increase in real income for the household. So, as remuneration goes up, more or less permanently, in one area of the world-economy, it is compensated in terms of the world-economy as a whole by the appearance of new cohorts of workers who will accept lower remuneration for the identical work, holding of course efficiency constant.

The problem with this solution to the regularly repeated problem of the owner/producers is that after 25-50 years the workers in this new zone of production are able to overcome their initial urban disorientation and political ignorance and proceed down the same path of class struggle as did others previously in other areas of the world. The zone in question thereupon ceases to be a zone of historically-lower remuneration, or at least not to the same degree. Sooner or later, the employers are required, in their self-interest, to flee again, relocating to yet another zone. This constant geographical shift of the zones of production has worked quite well over the centuries, but does have an Achilles heel. The world is running out of new zones into which to relocate. This is what we mean by the de-ruralization of the world, which is going on apace, and at a very accelerated rate since 1945. The proportion of world population that lives in cities went from 30 to 60 percent between 1950 and 2000.[24] The capitalist world-economy should run out of such zones entirely within 25 years at the most. There are already too few. And with modern means of communication, the time period for new zones to learn the lessons of how to organize has been drastically reduced. Hence, the ability of employers to keep remuneration in check has been drastically curtailed.

The costs of inputs are dependent on what percentage of the inputs the employer is required to pay. To the extent that he can get inputs free, his costs remain low. The major mechanism by which employers have over the centuries been able to avoid payment for inputs is by shifting the cost to others. This is called the externalization of costs. The three principal costs that have been externalized are detoxification, renewal of primary resources, and infrastructure.

Detoxification is easy to handle in the beginning. One dumps waste somewhere that is public or unoccupied. This costs next to nothing. The costs are usually not immediate, but delayed. The eventual difficulties become the problem of the "public"—either as individuals or collectively as governments. Clean-up, when it is undertaken, is seldom paid for by the original user. In pre-modern times, rulers moved to different castles as they ran out of sewage dumps. In the capitalist world-economy, producers do more or less the same. The problem here is identical to the problem of runaway factories and remuneration levels. We are running out of new prospective dumps. In addition, the collective cost of toxification has caught up with us, or at least we are more aware of it because of scientific advances. Hence, the world seeks to detoxify waste. This is called concern with the ecology. And as concern mounts, the question of who pays comes to the forefront. There is increasing pressure to make the user of the resources who leaves toxic waste pay the costs of detoxification. This is called internalization of costs. To the extent that governments impose such internalization of costs, the overall costs of production rise, sometimes quite steeply.

The issue of the renewal of primary resources is basically analogous. If forests are cut down, they may renew themselves via natural processes, but often slowly. And the faster forests are cut down (because of increased world production), the harder it is for the natural renewal process to take place in meaningful time. So here too, as the ecological concerns have come to the fore, both governments and social actors have put pressure on users either to restrain use or to invest in renewal. And to the extent that governments impose internalization of these costs, the costs of production rise.

Finally, the same is true of infrastructure. Infrastructure, almost by definition, is expenditure on costly activities that cannot be attributed to a single producer—for example, constructing public roadways over which transportation of goods takes place. But the fact that these costs cannot be considered the costs of a single producer does not mean that they cannot be considered the costs of a multitude of producers. Furthermore, the cost of such infrastructure has escalated geometrically. Yes, they are public goods, but the public can be specified up to a point. And once again, to the extent that governments impose even partial internalization of such costs, the costs of production rise.

The third basic cost of production is taxation. Any comparison of the total level of taxation in the world, or in any part of the world, with the world of a century ago reveals that everyone is paying higher taxes today, whatever the oscillation of the rates. What accounts for this? There are three major expenditures of all governments—the costs of collective security (armies, police, etc.); the costs of all kinds of public welfare; and the costs of administration (most importantly, the costs of collecting the taxes). Why have these costs of government risen so steeply?

The costs of security have risen simply as a result of technological advance. The toys security forces use are every day in every way more expensive. After all, security is a game in which all sides always try to have more than their opponents. It is like an endless auction in which the bids are always being raised. Perhaps if we had a generalized nuclear holocaust, and the surviving world went back to bows and arrows, these costs would go down. But in the wake of anything less, I see no way to expect such a reduction.

In addition, the costs of welfare have been going up steadily and nothing is slowing them down, despite all the hoopla about doing that. They are going up for three reasons. The first is that the politics of the capitalist world-economy have pushed the dominant strata to make concessions to the dangerous classes, who have been demanding three things—education, health services, and guarantees of lifelong income. Furthermore, the level of the demands has been going up steadily and becoming more geographically extensive. In addition, people are living longer (partly the consequence of precisely these welfare measures), and hence the collective costs have increased because of the increase in the number of beneficiaries. The second reason is that advances in technology in education and health have increased the costs of providing the appropriate machinery (just as in the case of expenditures on security). And finally, the producers in each of these domains have taken advantage of this government-subsidized public demand to take a big cut of the pie.

Welfare, as the conservative complaint has said, has become an entitlement. And it is difficult to see how any government could survive a truly significant cutback in these expenditures. But of course, someone must pay for this. And producers in the end pay, either directly or via their employees who demand higher remuneration precisely to pay these costs.

We do not have good data on the steady increase of all these costs, but they are considerable. On the other hand, we cannot have a rise in the sales price of world goods to match the increase of production costs precisely because of the enormous expansion of world production which has reduced the multiple monopolizations and increased world competition. So, the bottom line is that the costs of production have risen faster than the sales prices of production, and this means a profit squeeze, which translates into difficulties in accumulating capital through production. This squeeze has been evident overall for some thirty years already which accounts for the speculative rage that has encompassed world capitalists since the 1970s and which shows no signs of letting up. But bubbles burst. Balloons cannot be infinitely expanded.

To be sure, capitalists collectively fight back. This is what neoliberal globalization is all about—a massive political attempt to roll back remuneration costs, to counter demands for internalization of costs, and of course to reduce levels of taxation. As has happened with every previous such counteroffensive against rising costs, it has succeeded partially, but only very partially. Even after all the cutbacks by the most reactionary regimes, the costs of production in the first decade of the twenty-first century are markedly higher than they were in 1945. I think of this as the ratchet effect—two steps forward and one step backward add up to a secular rising curve.

As the underlying economic structures of the capitalist world-economy have been moving in the direction of reaching an asymptote which makes it increasingly difficult to accumulate capital, the

AFTER DEVELOPMENTALISM AND GLOBALIZATION, WHAT?

political structures that have been holding the dangerous classes in check have also run into trouble.

The period of developmentalism, 1945-1970, was also the period of the triumph of the historic antisystemic movements, which came into power in one form or another almost everywhere. Their biggest promise had been the developmentalist dream. When that failed, the support of their followers disintegrated. The movements, whether they called themselves communist or social-democrat or national liberation movements, fell from power almost everywhere. The period of globalization, 1970-2000, was the period of deep disillusionment with the historic antisystemic movements. They fell from grace, and are unlikely to attract the deep loyalty of the mass of the populations again. They may be supported elect orally as better than the other guys, but they no longer are deemed worthy of the faith they represented for a golden future.

The decline of these movements—the so-called Old Left—is not in fact a plus for the smooth functioning of the capitalist world-economy. While these movements were antisystemic in their goals, they were disciplined structures which controlled the spontaneous radical impulses of their followers. They mobilized for specific actions, but they also demobilized followers, especially when they were in government, insisting on the benefits in a distant future, as opposed to untrammeled disturbances in the present. The collapse of these movements represents the collapse on constraints on the dangerous classes, who thereby become dangerous again. The spreading anarchy of the twenty-first century is the clear reflection of this shift.

The capitalist world-economy is today a very unstable structure. It has never been more so. It is very vulnerable to sudden and swift destructive currents.

III

"If it is not, what kinds of alternatives present themselves to all of us now?"

It is not very comforting to anyone in countries of the South to say that the present world-system is in structural crisis and that we are in a transition from it to some other world-system over the next 25-50 years. They will want to know what happens in the meantime, and what if anything they can or should do to improve the lot of the populations of these countries right now. People tend to live in the present, as indeed they should. On the other hand, it is important to know what are the constraints of the present in order that our actions be maximally useful, in the sense that they further the objectives we seek in some meaningful way. So, let me indicate what I think is the scenario over the next 25-50 years, and what that implies for the immediate present.

The scenario over the next 25-50 years is twofold. On the one hand, the collapse of our existing historical system is most likely for all the reasons I laid out just previously. On the other hand, what will replace the existing system is completely uncertain, inherently unpredictable, although all of us can have input into that uncertain outcome. It is inherently uncertain because, whenever we are in a systemic bifurcation, there is no way of knowing in advance which fork in the road we shall collectively take. This is the message of the sciences of complexity.[25]

On the other hand, precisely because this is a period of transition in which the existing system is far from equilibrium, with wild and chaotic oscillations in all domains, the pressures to return to equilibrium are extremely weak. This means that, in effect, we are in the domain of "free will" and therefore our actions, individual and collective, have a direct and large impact on the historical choices with which the world is faced. In a sense, to translate this into our concerns, we may say that the objective of "development" which countries and scholars have been pursuing for some fifty years now are far more realizable in the next 25-50 years than they ever were up to now. But of course there is no guarantee, for the outcome is uncertain.

In the larger geopolitical arena, there are presently three principal cleavages. There is first the triadic struggle between the United States, western Europe, and Japan/East Asia to be the principal locus of capital accumulation in the capitalist world-economy. There is secondly the long-standing struggle between North and South for distribution of the world surplus. And there is the new struggle that revolves around the structural crisis of the capitalist world-economy and centers on which of the two possible forks the world will take in completing the transition to a new system.

The first two struggles are traditional within the framework of the modern world-system. The so-called triad are roughly equal contestants in the attempt to reorganize the world-system's production and financial systems. As with all such triadic struggles, there is pressure to reduce the triad to a dyad, which may occur in the next decade or so. I have long argued that the most likely pair is the United States and Japan/East Asia against western Europe/Russia.[26] But I shall not repeat this argument here, since I consider this struggle secondary to the issue of overcoming the polarization of the existing system, that is, permitting what we have called "development" throughout the world-system.

The second struggle, that between North and South, has of course been a central focus of development issues for the last fifty years. Indeed, the great difference between the era of developmentalism and the era of globalization has been the relative strength of the two sides. While in the first era, the South seemed to be improving its position, if only slightly, the second period has been one of a triumphant pushback by the North. But this pushback has now come to a close, with the deadlock in the World Trade Organization and the split among the spokesmen of the North about the wisdom of the Washington Consensus. I think here of the increasingly open dissent of such figures as Joseph Stiglitz, Jeffrey Sachs, and George Soros, among many others, and the remarkable softening of the rigidities of the International Monetary Fund in the post-2000 period. I do not expect that in the coming decades there will be much push off-center in this contest.

It is the third cleavage which reflects the new situation, that of the structural crisis with its consequent chaos in the world-system and the bifurcation that is occurring. This is the split between the spirit of Davos and the spirit of Porto Alegre, which I mentioned previously. I should explain what I think are the central issues here. The struggle is not about whether or not we are in favor of capitalism as a world-system. The struggle is about what should replace it, given the implosion of the present world-system. The two replacement possibilities have no real names and have no detailed outlines. What is in question is essentially whether the replacement system will be hierarchical and polarizing (that is, like the present system, or worse) or will be instead relatively democratic and egalitarian. These are basic moral choices, and being on one side of the other dictates our politics.

The contours of the actual political players are still uncertain. The side of the spirit of Davos is split between those whose vision of the future involves an unremitting harshness of strategy and institution-building and those who insist that such a vision would create an untenable system, which could not last. At the moment, it is a very divided camp. The side of the spirit of Porto Alegre has other problems. They constitute politically merely a loose alliance of variegated movements all over the world which, today at least, meet together within the framework of the World Social Forum (WSF). Collectively, they have no clear strategy as yet. But they do have a good deal of grassroots support, and they are clear about what they oppose.

The question is what those who would uphold the spirit of Porto Alegre should really do to advance this "other world" they assert is possible. And this is a double question. What is it that those few governments who share their vision, at least up to a point, should do, and what the multiple movements should do. Governments deal with the short-run issues. Movements can deal with both short-run and middle-run issues. Both kinds of issues affect the longer run transition process. And short-run issues affect our daily lives immediately. An intelligent political strategy must move on all fronts at once.

The biggest short-run issue is the continuing drive of the neoliberal globalizers to achieve a one-sided expansion of open borders—open in the South, but not really open in the North. This is the heart of the persistent discussion within the framework of the World Trade Organization, and of all the bilateral discussions being conducted most notably by the United States but also secondarily by the European Union and its members—the creation of multiple "free trade agreements" like NAFTA, CAFTA, etc. Basically what the United States pushes for is guarantees for its monopolies (so-called intellectual property) and access for its financial institutions in return for limited tariff concessions on agricultural and low-value industrial goods produced in countries of the South.

The offensive within the WTO was stalled at Cancun by a coalition of medium powers of the South—Brazil, India, South Africa, etc.—who put forward a simple demand: free trade that works both ways. If the North wants us to open our borders to them, they said in effect, it must open its borders to us. But the North is basically unable to accept this kind of deal for two reasons. It would result in considerably increased unemployment and downsized income in countries of the North, which is politically impossible for governments subject to electoral contests to accept. And it is not clear to the triad which of them would profit most, or lose least, from such arrangements, and therefore they hesitate. After all, the triad is engaged with tariff/subsidy controversies with each other, and arrangements with the South would weaken their political positions in this economically even more important conflict from the point of view of the countries of the North.

One can draw two conclusions from this. This is a political quarrel doomed to a standstill. And it is politically very important for the countries of the South to maintain this stance, from their own point of view. This is the single most important action these governments can take to further the possibility of maintaining or raising the standard of living in their countries. To the sirens of the neoliberal dogmas, these countries are now responding skeptically, show me, and this skepticism is justified.

Of course, these governments have to remain in power. And the biggest threat to that is external interference in their politics. What the larger countries of the South are now doing, and will speed up doing in the next decade, is seeking to enter the nuclear club. What this will accomplish is to largely neutralize external military threat, and thereby minimize external political threat. And the third thing one can demand of these governments is social welfare distribution within their countries, which of course could include low-level development projects (such as digging wells, etc.) What one cannot expect of these countries is that some policy on their part is going to turn them into a Denmark in the next 10-20-30 years. It's not going to happen, and is basically a diversion from an intelligent policy. The role of progressive governments is primarily to make sure that conditions in their countries and the world do not get still worse in the decades to come.

It is the movements that can do more than the governments, although the movements need to keep minimally progressive governments in power, and not engage in leftist infantilist critiques about the lack of achievements that are in fact impossible to expect. And here we must point out an important element that is often lost from observation. The first two geopolitical cleavages are geographic: conflicts among the Triad; North-South conflicts. But the conflict between the spirit of Davos and the spirit of Porto Alegre has no geography. It cuts across the entire world, as do the movements. It is a class struggle, a moral struggle, not a geographic struggle.

In the medium run, what the movements can best do is to push decommodification wherever they can, and to the extent that they can. No one can be quite sure how this would work. It will take a lot of experimentation to find viable formulas. And such experimentation is going on. It is going on, we must remember, within a basically hostile environment, in which there are systemic pressures to undermine any such attempts, and which can corrupt the participants with not too much difficulty. But decommodification not only stems the drive for neoliberal extensions but builds the basis for an alternate political culture.

Of course, the theorists of capitalism have long derided decommodification, arguing that it is illusory, that it goes against some presumed innate social psychology of humankind, that it is inefficient, and that it guarantees lack of economic growth and therefore of poverty. All of this is false. We have only to look at two major institutions of the modern world—universities and hospitals—to realize that, at least up to twenty years ago, no one questioned that they should be run as non-profit institutions, without shareholders or profit-takers. And it would be hard to argue seriously that, for that reason, they have been inefficient, unreceptive to technological advances, incapable of attracting competent personnel to run them, or unable to perform the basic services for which they were created.

We don't know how these principles would work, if applied to large-scale production like steel production or small-scale, more artisanal production. But to dismiss this out of hand is simply blind. And in an era when productive enterprises are becoming far less profitable than previously, precisely because of the economic growth which the capitalist world-economy has bred, is foolish. Pushing alternate forms of development along these lines has a potential for answering problems not only of the South but of the declining industrial regions of the North.

In any case, as I have insisted, the issue is not what will magically solve the immediate dilemmas of our world-system but the basis on which we shall create the successor world-system. And to address that seriously, we must first of all comprehend with some clarity the historical development of our present system, appreciate its structural dilemmas today, and open our mind to radical alternatives for the future. And we must do all this, not merely academically but practically, that is, living in the present, and concerned with the immediate needs of people as well as longer-run transformations. We must therefore fight both defensively and offensively. And if we do it well, we may, but only may, come out ahead in the lifetimes of some of the younger members of this audience.

7

NAMING GROUPS: THE POLITICS OF CATEGORIZING AND IDENTITIES[27]

Something called political economy has long existed, but it needs to be rethought in terms of new categories. Our task begins with the question, what was the old political economy that needs rethinking? It was first of all about the "wealth of nations," to remember how Adam Smith formulated it. Marx didn't like the term; he wrote a "critique of political economy." Marx was especially unhappy that what was called political economy lacked a discussion of the centrality of class and class conflict. With the departmentalization of the social sciences in the second half of the nineteenth century, the term disappeared. Political economists began to call themselves economists, and a new term—political science, or government—came on the scene to pick up the slack.

In the 1960s, there was a revival of the term, political economy. It began to be used by Marxists or quasi-Marxists who wanted to talk about class and class conflict as the basis of politics, but who were shy about using the term, Marxism. In the 1970s, market fundamentalist economists also revived the term because they wanted to show how the political arena could be analyzed in terms of purely market-oriented characteristics. Between the left and the right, the center was vanquished and the term came back into accepted usage—accepted usage, but not at all an accepted definition.

At approximately the same time, social movements were pushing the issues of race and gender to the forefront of political debate. With-in the university, one of the major intellectual targets of those raising the issues of race and gender was the neglect of these categories by both the old version of political economy and the revived version. One major consequence was that race and gender became instituted as newly-framed categories of social science.

In the academy, this insistence on the centrality of race and gender took the form of creating new programs/departments, new journals, and new scholarly associations. In the 1970s, these new structures became heavily dominated by a concern for analyzing and affirming identities, which in turn tended to breed a spirit of organizational, intellectual, and political separatism. By the 1980s, the various structures that had by then been created were beset by internal debates, some quite ferocious, about omissions caused by the separatism. Some women began to complain that race-centered groupings neglected the issue of gender. And some people of color began to complain that gender-centered groupings neglected the issue of race. And within both sets of groupings, there were others who complained about the neglect of class.

So, by the 1990s, it began to be quite standard to talk of the threesome—race, class, gender—as a complex set of interwoven central categories, all of which had to be addressed by serious social scientists. Of course, the list is not complete. There are other candidates for inclusion in such a list, such as sexuality, age, various kinds of disabilities, and an ever-expanding list of others.

Nation is a slightly different kind of category. Political economists—the early and the recent versions—simply assumed that what they were discussing took place within the state, the state that was a nation. But states have had a bad habit of not being truly homogeneous, and hence from time to time social scientists discussed a vague category called ethnic groups, a term that was for a long time only applied to non-dominant groups and, in the United States at least, was somehow distinguished from racial categories. We are now however much more aware that there is no such thing as a homogeneous state, that every state has groups within it which we can call ethnic groups, and that socially such ethnic groups are always ranked on a prestige and privilege ladder within the state.

And then too, let us not forget, there is religion as the basis of identity. In this first decade of the twenty-first century, how can we possibly ignore the thrust forward as political categories of religious identities, quite often in the form of so-called fundamentalist movements? This recrudescence of the centrality of religious identification seems to be quite global, occurring everywhere and within all religious traditions.

So, we have a cornucopia of categories that are being proposed to us. In addition, many of those proposing these categories insist that they are not at all primordial, or essential, but socially-constructed. Well, if they are socially constructed (for which a good case can be made), then of course they can be socially reconstructed as often as some set of persons wishes to try to do so. Furthermore, there are al-ways two sides to any social construction—those who propose them-selves as a category and the others not in this category who may or may not be willing to recognize the self-proclaimed group as a social category.

This need for at least partial reciprocity of perception is no doubt what is behind the loudness of the demands made by proponents of a new term for a particular social category; they are seeking recognition of the category by the others. And this brings us to the phenomenon which is not the least of our problems. The names for social categories keep changing. A group that demands more rights than it is presently being accorded by the others frequently feels that the language the others use to describe it is pejorative and therefore seeks to reframe their status by employing a new term, and demanding that others employ it as well. But any new term that is widely adopted fairly quickly comes to be perceived as pejorative as well, and proponents go on to still another term. A simple illustration: in the United States, the descendants of enslaved Africans were first called "nigger" or "darkie," then "black," then "colored people" (remember the National Association for the Advancement of Colored People), then "negro," then "Negro" (remember the National Negro Congress), then "Afro-American," then "Black" (remember Black

Panthers), then "African-American," and tomorrow who knows? It seems a never-ending swirl.

So we have two problems here. The first is what kinds of groups are important analytically and politically, and what are their boundaries? And the second is what is the terminology we should use to refer to them, and why is this important?

GROUPS AND THEIR BOUNDARIES

The first thing to ask about a group, a question rarely posed as a question, is where is it? Groups are located—not only located geographically, but located historically as well (which includes their geography), and not least located morally.

The moral location is at once obvious and yet seldom really debated. Almost all people believe, and say, that their own group is good if not the best (and thereby implicitly that other groups are not good, or at least less good, or maybe even bad). Anthropologists have long pointed out that the names we give to so-called tribal peoples are usually the term they have in their own language for "people," implying that others are not people. China, in Chinese, is the Middle Kingdom, that is, the center of the world. And the United States, its presidents regularly repeat, is "the greatest country in the world."

So in moral terms, almost all of us prefer to be "we" rather than "they." And we seem to think that "they" all, or almost all, would prefer to become "we." This, of course, becomes a major element in the recurring, and often vicious, debates about immigration policy in country after country. The idea that we might place all peoples/nations/states on a scale of perfect moral equity seems to most people perverse, even demented. Yet the data for any alternative position is remarkably weak, indeed virtually absent, as any serious social scientist can tell us. But in this moral debate, social science is remarkably absent, largely out of fear that it might suffer the slings and arrows of passionate repression. Soldiers and clerics are sometimes courageous; social scientists usually prefer to take refuge in claiming to be objective.

The moral affirmation of a group quite frequently determines its definition of geographic location. Many kinds of groups lay claim to rights over space. And their definitions of spatial rights are often excessive, from the point of view of neighbors as well as of less-interested observers. It is quite easy to discover, or even invent outright, historic claims of ownership. There are political debates which are turned into a contest between the data of my archaeologists against those of your archaeologists, as though a pile of artifacts were a legitimate basis for contemporary moral decisions. I suppose, now that we know that all of *homo sapiens* are descended from a small group of people who were located somewhere in eastern Africa many millennia ago, that Kenya (perhaps in conjunction with some neighbors) might be entitled to claim the territory of the entire world.

Nonetheless, geography is central to the life of groups—certainly to nations, states, races, and even religions. And since geographic location is a constantly evolving and displacing phenomenon, we need to regard geography historically. And when we do that, we have to decide if the space location simply changes with the times, or the true spatial location is the widest zone that one can construct out of historical data, or perhaps the optimal zone in terms of contemporary geopolitics.

One should note that gender is the one category that has no geopolitical space. Men and women are found everywhere in roughly equal proportions, and as far as we know always have been and always will be. To be sure, we can construct ghettos within the outer geopolitical space. This is what we do when a community restricts the movement of women outside the defined household zone, or when we assign boys and girls to separate institutional structures. When such ghettoization is intensive, it seems be an egalitarian demand to call for dismantlement of the ghettos. But as one begins to dismantle them, there are those among the erstwhile lower-status group (and this applies not only to gender but to race/ethnic groups as well) who seek to recreate the ghettos on the grounds that ghettos strengthen identification and serve to prepare persons for battle in the wider social arena.

Wherever and whenever there is a group, there is a counter-group, both from the point of view of the group and of the counter-group. A group of any kind is a relational concept, not an analytic essence. Since all groups are socially created, they are socially created for some purpose. And the purpose is to advance the rights (and privileges) of the group. It is therefore inevitably the case that doing this is at the expense of some other group. Equalization diminishes the advantage of those who had it, and only saintly persons strip themselves voluntarily of advantage, whatever their moral codes.

Once the group and counter-group are established as significant entities, with members ready to affirm their membership and struggle for the objectives of the group, we then have a political reality of that moment. To understand its import and its importance, we must immediately look beyond the contested terrain, as defined by the group and the counter-group. Their definition of the terrain of struggle is self-interested, but is itself part of the parameters of the struggle. Both the analyst and the moralist must take account of these definitions and seek to understand their meanings and their subtexts.

Nonetheless, both the analysis and the moral judgment require placing the socio-political encounter of the group and its counter-group within the entire social context of the world-system. There is no way in which the contested terrain can be treated as an isolated phenomenon on its own terms. If ever the so-called butterfly effect can be seen to be important, it is in this contested terrain. Whatever is done anywhere affects this terrain and the struggle therein. The geography of the terrain and the moral meaning of the struggle are virtually at the mercy of the entire world-system.

And yet, by and large, almost all of the pertinent action is in the hands of the group and the counter-group within the existing terrain. The role of so-called outside intruders is vastly overstated. The outside intruders act simply by existing and by pursuing their own objectives elsewhere. Still they are very real. And those who neglect analyzing them and evaluating them are poor describers and ineffective actors.

History is our poorest guide for understanding the terms of the debate. History is one of the tools of the actors, but seldom one of the basic motives for the current struggle. The appeal to history is in large part a search for contemporary alliances. It may not at all be true that group X and Y were allied centuries ago. Rather it serves both X and Y today to believe that they were allied centuries ago. The asserted history justifies the present alliance. And because this history is almost an invention, it is ephemeral. We are constantly amazed at the redrawing of alliances in all these contested terrains. But the alliances are being redrawn because of the evolution of something or other in the wider world-system—the butterfly effect.

Shifting alliances in turn lead to shifting definitions of the boundaries. How local, regional, or transregional we wish to define the location of a group, our group or the other group, is a function of the political alliances we are creating and recreating constantly. This is not a question of hypocrisy, but of geopolitical tactics. Everyone is engaged in the same game, and charges of hypocrisy are not serious moral accusations but for the most part merely a weapon in the struggle within the terrain.

Are some kinds of groups more important than others? The hierarchy of types of groups is in constant evolution as well. Whether we give primacy to class, to race, to gender, to combinations thereof, or to anything else is itself a political issue. To understand why we do so, we have to analyze the present. To assess whether particular priorities are appropriate is to assess our strategy and its efficacy in achieving our goals. To analyze what groups do and which kinds of groups achieve priority status is a primary task of ongoing social science. To assess which kinds of groups ought to be given priority is a primary task of our moral judgment. It is a primary task and a very complex one. It cannot be undertaken lightly, since the consequences of appropriate analysis and judgment are very serious. Politics may be a game, but it is a deadly game from which none of us can escape.

TERMINOLOGY AND ITS PITFALLS

Terminology matters. No one should know this better than social scientists, who are constantly inventing concepts to legitimate what they are saying and to channel the general discussion. However, as we also know, terminology is a slippery tool. Words are not copyrighted. And we all can give a word whatever meaning or tonality we wish. And we all do precisely that all the time. A very large part of what we call theorizing is really conceptualizing, and it's a very subjective task.

Gertrude Stein told us that "a rose is a rose is a rose." But one of my teachers once told me that "a State is not *un État* is not *ein Staat*." Which is it, then? If I told you to choose between "A woman is a woman is a woman," and "a woman is not *une femme* is not *ein Frau*," which would you think more correct? The answer, for me at least, is that we have, at the very least, to analyze the context in which these statements are made, and the functions they serve within that context.

Terminology for groups is always defensive and most often aggressive as well. Take pejorative terms we use about others. We are all familiar with most of the current ones, at least in our own environs. And we can usually spot the pejorative character of terms we may hear for the first time. When Sen. George Allen in his electoral contest encountered a cameraman who was filming his meeting on behalf of his opponent, a cameraman who was a South Asian by origin or ethnicity, he called him publicly a "macaca." Virtually no one in the audience knew the exact meaning or origin of that term. They and the rest of us would all to be educated by subsequent media reports that the term was used as a slur in French-speaking colonial Africa and that it meant "monkey." But before knowing that, we had all already sensed that it must have been pejorative.

The immediate consequences of using that term were first of all a public analysis of the term, secondly a widespread report of earlier usage by Sen. Allen of other racially pejorative terms, thirdly a denial by Sen. Allen that he had intended to be pejorative, and fourthly, a decline in public support for Sen. Allen because of belief that he did indeed intend to be pejorative. So what have we here? A term that was a slur was used in public. It probably was intended to appeal to negative sentiments about people of color. But the use of the slur was dangerous political tactics since it violated a public norm against using such slurs, a public norm that is indeed fairly recent in U.S. history. About Sen. Allen, the post-usage political analysis has to have been, did he gain or lose more votes in using the term?

But what makes a term pejorative? It is a matter of social perception. A term is deemed pejorative if it fulfils minimally two characteristics: it differs from the most obvious, socially-legitimate term one could use, and it is intended to degrade the group described. But power contexts vary. There are those contexts in which the dominant group feels free to use pejoratives and the dominated group feels it has no immediate alternative but to suffer their usage, since protesting the usage would lead to severe repressive tactics.

But there are of course other contexts in which overt usage of pejoratives is deemed violating norms of equality or tolerance. In these cases, the usage may continue, but at a diminished rate and more privately. Still the attitudes may still be much the same. And covert usage (for example, "monkey" in a foreign language) may signal the same intent and the same call for a particular socio-political alliance. But since it violates ostensible norms, one has to deny pejorative intent. It's a sort of winking phenomenon, which works up to a point. But only up to a point, as Sen. Allen discovered.

Pejoratives however are easy to discern and to discredit. There are subtler and perhaps even more important social struggles over terminology. Take the campaign, launched more or less about 1970 by feminists, over the use of masculine pronouns to refer to prestigious positions. This is a problem that does not occur in all languages, which have different rules about the use of pronouns. For example, in French, the pronominal adjective can be masculine or feminine. But which it is, is determined not by the person to whom one is referring but to the gender of the noun that is being modified. This however is not true in English, and hence the start of a big campaign and for a while a big controversy about the gender of pronouns.

Basically, in English, historically the masculine pronoun has been used as a generic pronoun. In many situations, it was presumed that "he" meant "he or she." This is also true of many occupational terms which tended to end in "-man." Of course, as feminists pointed out, the assumption was that the pronoun or the occupational term was referring to positions from which women were largely or even entirely excluded. The feminists argued that such usage had major social consequences of various kinds. It socialized children into assuming that women were not apt for certain positions. It signaled to corporate structures that women should not rise to high status (or recompense) within these positions, or that they were inherently less competent.

What followed was a campaign by feminists to change social usage, that is, to get everyone to be conscious of the illegitimacy of the generic masculine. Thirty years later, one can say that this campaign has largely succeeded, at least in many parts of the world. In spoken and written English, there is today a good deal of consciousness concerning the gender of pronouns.

But what is the alternative to the generic masculine? Given the syntax of English, it has not been easy to agree on one. One alternative is to shift from the singular to the plural, since in English the plural "they" has no gender. Another is to find substitute occupational terms—"mail carrier" in place of "postman," for example. A third is using the passive voice (otherwise frowned upon) because it lends itself to easier avoidance of the issue. A fourth is to invent new non-gender-specific pronouns (which however have never caught on).

A similar issue, posed in a different fashion, is the use of capitalization. Again this is a problem for English. In German all nouns are capitalized. In French, while geographic nouns are capitalized, names of groups are not, and even geographical names are not capitalized when used as adjectives. English usage is in-between. English distinguishes between common and proper nouns, the latter being capitalized. The corresponding adjectives follow the same distinction.

In the United States, the names of social groups based on religion, ethnicity, or nationality are all capitalized—Catholics, Latinos, Hungarians. The only groups about which there has been an issue have been racial groups. The term "colored people" was never capitalized.

The term "negro" was not capitalized for a very long time. It took *The New York Times* some 60-70 years to decide that it warranted a capital. When "Negro" was cast aside in favor of "black," *The New York Times*, and just about everyone else, refused to capitalize it. The use of the capital remains an issue. Thus, it is common for writers, whether in the media or in scholarly work, to put together a string of groups in one sentence, in which every term is capitalized except "blacks."

The campaign against the generic masculine in English and the campaign to capitalize. "Blacks" are both meaningful campaigns, with significant social consequences. But winning a terminological campaign, while important, can be momentary. When Negroes decided that they preferred to be called Blacks, they immediately lost the capitalization and had to start that battle over again. Groups have their enemies, and their enemies are seldom quiescent.

WHERE DO WE GO FROM HERE?

I believe we have a starting-point in something that Joan Smith wrote in her marvelous and little-known essay entitled, "We Irish Women: Gender, History, and the World-Economy":

> Women's historical experiences cannot be reduced to that of men. Of that there is no question. It is exactly this truism that supports the contention that without women as historical subjects, there is no accurate historical account. But this does not at all mean that women's history can be treated as conceptually and empirically independent of the institutional and structural changes that constitute the historical moment. Without history, there are no women. But without women, there is no history.[28]

It is in the light of this reminder—that we mutually construct each other—that I believe we have to build our engaged scholarship on a set of premises.

The first premise is that we have to be very careful when we categorize groups and assert identities. These conceptual activities are crude tools and are seldom helpful if we wish to engage in fine-tuned political analysis and activity. For one thing, any argument we make can almost always be used against us in turn.

The second premise is that we have to be very careful when we assert priorities, particularly priorities in being victims of the powerful. It is usually wiser for the weak to be empathetic with each other, even if (or should I say especially if) one weak group is seen to be oppressing another weaker group.

The third premise is that the first step in a serious analysis is to keep our eye on the ball, on who are really powerful in any existing geopolitical and geo-cultural context, and how they profit from (or fail to profit from) our processes of categorizing and asserting identities.

"Without history, there are no [classes, races, genders, nations]."[29] What does this mean, in practice? The first thing it means is that these categories are all relational, not essential. E. P. Thompson told us that the English working class was "made." Yes, and it was made at a certain point in time, as a result of particular historical processes and in response to particular power configurations in the world-system as a whole and in a particular nation at that time.

Individuals and households have of course multiple identities. They therefore are shifting their priorities among their identities constantly, indeed frequently. There are no false identities, only false denial of identities. The identities conferred upon us by others are unavoidable and impossible to erase. But we can react to these impositions of priorities in various ways—accepting them, rejecting the priorities, or adopting the multiple in-between nuanced positions. Both the impositions and the reactions are political acts, to be analyzed in their context, to be assessed in terms of our moral evaluations, to be subject to criticism as useful political strategies.

"But without [classes, races, genders, nations], there is no history."[30] These categories are useful only insofar as they explain what has historically occurred, is occurring, and will probably continue to occur (at least for some time). We can individually be exasperated with this or that assertion of this or that identity, because we think the assertions are exaggerated, or because they neglect other categories which seem to us more relevant in a particular situation, or because they fail to give others the benefit of the same doubt that they insist be given to themselves. A lot of the debate about affirmative action is of precisely this variety.

But the bottom line is always that there do exist structural modes of discrimination, mistreatment, and oppression, as well of course as overt and formal modes. And it is always an essential element in diminishing this oppression that some given group assert its anger, its self-consciousness, and its right to equality in every respect. The exaggerations are less important than the oppressions.

We are living in a time of a long historic transition from our existing world-system, the capitalist world-economy, to something else, which may or may not be better, when a new world order is finally established. This is a time of fundamental struggle worldwide about our future, a very uncertain future. I have called this in previous writings the struggle between the spirit of Davos and the spirit of Porto Alegre. Davos refers to the World Economic Forum which has existed since the 1970s as the annual meeting-ground of the world's elites—businessmen, politicians, journalists, and Establishment intellectuals. They come together each year fundamentally to try to work out a strategy—not to preserve the existing system but to ensure that it will be replaced by one that maintains its basic features, that of a system based on a hierarchy of privilege and inequality of reward.

Porto Alegre refers to the World Social Forum (WSF), which met for the first time in that Brazilian city in 2001 and which has established itself as the anti-Davos. It is defined as an open forum for all those movements throughout the world who believe that "another world is possible" and who are committed minimally to opposition to a neoliberal version of globalization and to imperialism in all its forms. Its goal is the opposite of that of Davos. Its goal is to create a non-polarized world order based on relative equality and relative democracy.

It is in the World Social Forum, however, that all the contradictions of the processes of categorizing and the claims of identity get acted out. Participants in the WSF now number over 100,000 persons in its world meetings. And who are these people? They come from every conceivable kind of antisystemic movement. These movements are diverse in their geographical scope—some international, some regional, some national, some local. They are diverse in their social com-position—some based on class, some based on race, some based on gender, some based on nation. And they are diverse in their primary (or immediate) objectives. Some seek to defend workers' rights. Some are concerned primarily with issues of the environment. Some are peasant or rural movements. Some are organizations of indigenous peoples who do not have full rights in their countries. Some are concerned with problems of health or access to water.

You can see that this could be a veritable Babel. And since the structure of the WSF is that it has no officers, makes no policy statements, and even has no spokespersons, there cannot be any top-down mode of keeping such a world congress clearly focused. On the contrary, it now has a structure which allows the groups, from the bottom, to propose themes for panels they will organize. And there are perhaps 40-60 such panels going on in any given time slot at the meetings.

But the object of the exercise is threefold: to allow a mutually educative interchange between activists of every possible kind and geographic location; to instill a sense of empathetic respect among these movements; to encourage emergent political action that will have some real impact on the world struggle. Does it work? This is precisely what the WSF will be debating at its sixth such world meeting, in Nairobi in January 2007. For there are some who say that the great contribution of the WSF is precisely to have created a horizontal, non-hierarchical structure, unlike all the many failed internationals. And there are those who argue precisely the opposite, that too much horizontalism has led to mere rhetoric and impeded effective action.

Underlying this debate is the sense of those who insist on the horizontal mode that this is the only way to be inclusive of all the oppressed groups throughout the world. And underlying the discomfort of those who criticize this mode is the sense that only a resurrected vertical structure which precisely does exclude some of these groups can in the end be politically efficacious. The latter are often those who give priority to workers' struggles. The former are often those who insist on the nonexistence of priorities among the various struggles.

One of the questions that pervades the organizational debates is what can actually unite a trade-union movement in eastern Europe, an ecology movement in Canada, a movement of peasant women in an African country, a movement for indigenous rights within India, and an anarchist youth movement in Latin America? And I leave out of the discussion the possible role of existing political parties in such an assemblage of movements.

Discussions about rethinking political economy are not merely abstract intellectual concerns. They have a very practical application to the central political struggles of our times. Furthermore, these struggles are not merely at the world level. For one of the consequences of the collapsing structure of the modern world-system, of the fact that we are living in a period of transition that may continue for another 20-40 years is that the world-system is fundamentally chaotic, with rather wide and swift fluctuations in the world-economy, and a considerable increase in the level of ongoing violence.

We discuss this all the time under the dubious label of "terrorism" as though the issue were that there exist a series of organizations (such as the by now virtually mythical Al-Qaeda), when the real issue is the collapse of internal social order in our various national states, as more and more people feel that they are actively living in a time of deep uncertainty beyond their control.

The political reaction to the fear generated by this uncertainty takes the form of civil strife, even civil war, in more and more parts of the world. Such civil strife is spreading. It is not restricted to a few places to which we give the silly label of "failed states." It is a phenomenon which is beginning to make its way into the heartlands of the dominant core zones of the world-system, into Western Europe and North America. And one of the key organizing ideas of civil strife is a form of identity politics which gets the label of the immigration issue. We see this going on everywhere in the political debates of the United States, of France, of Denmark, and indeed even of Japan, South Africa, and Mexico.

Protectionism may have many economic virtues. But, applied to social issues, to issues of identity, it has very few. We are engaged in a world struggle, not in a series of national struggles. And we will either formulate our strategies in terms of this world struggle or we shall lose the struggle. Given the continuing intensity of national identity—everywhere in the world, and not only in the United States—we have an uphill battle in reminding each other of the signal importance of class, race, and gender as central concerns in the search for a more egalitarian world-system.

I should like to conclude this discussion with another quote from the same article by Joan Smith:

> Gendered relationships do not meet world capitalism on the historical stage as though each are independent historical actors which, by virtue of their spatial and temporal co-existence, have the ability to influence each other. As we can see from considering the history of Ireland, the developments associated with the integration of that region into the world-economy are gendered, not because gendered relationships preceded these developments, but because the developments constituted the (re)creation of gender.... [G]ender has a world-historical character to it not because of some eternal patriarchy but because it is a part and parcel of world history.... Gender both contains within itself the history of the world and is an expression of that history as it developed in all of its specific forms.[31]

We are now in the process of creating a new world-system. How that new world-system constructs class, race, and gender is by no means a foregone conclusion. The new world order will emerge out of how we all choose among the historical options that will be presented to each of us. The struggle will be difficult. It may often be obscure. But it is very real. And what we need to make us strong is clarity of analysis, courage of moral judgment, and wisdom of political strategy. This is a tall order, but one we cannot avoid.

8

THE POLITICAL CONSTRUCTION OF ISLAM IN
THE MODERN WORLD-SYSTEM[32]

One has only to open today almost any newspaper published in the United States, Europe, or the Middle East (at least), and you will find some story about Islam, Islamists, or some other variant of this designation. I would remind you that had you done this same thing in the 1950s, the opposite would have been true. There were extremely few stories about Islam in the newspapers, even in the Middle East. What has changed? To understand the current situation, we have to trace the entire history of the political importance of religious affiliations in the modem world-system since the long sixteenth century.

THE MODERN WORLD-SYSTEM FROM 1500-1970

At the beginning, religious affiliations were politically extremely important. This was the era of the Reformation and the Counter-Reformation. Defining conflicts as those between Catholics and the others (Protestants, Anglicans, humanists, and in Spain Jews and Muslims) was central to political discourse. The political consequences included expulsions, civil wars, and persecutions. The Protestant-Catholic division was so pervasive and so profound that it could only be calmed somewhat by a political division of Europe under the slogan *cuius religio ehis regio*. This slogan, which meant that the religion of the ruler defined the state religion, was coined in the Peace of Augsburg in 1555 and was applied primarily to the Holy Roman Empire, which was the Germanic zone of Europe.

At the time, Europeans defined Islam as an extra-European force that was besieging Europe. The initial Muslim conquests of the eighth century in western Europe had reached Tours in France, and Muslim rulers governed almost all of what is today Spain for centuries, until they were finally totally expelled by the Christian forces of the *Reconquista* in 1492. But at just this time, the Ottoman Empire, a Muslim empire, expanded into Southeastern Europe, reaching its high point in the siege of Vienna in 1685. And of course the Ottomans remained in large parts of southeastern Europe right up until the end of the First World War.

European cultural history in the eighteenth and nineteenth centuries included a large measure of secularization of Christian states. In many countries, the internal religious conflict was now seen as Christians versus freethinkers, the latter trying to detach state institutions from their formal and informal links with Christian churches. Islam was scarcely noticed by Europeans at this time. It certainly was not the center of political debate or even discourse.

By the time we get to the twentieth century, one European state after another is ending or trying to end any political role for Christian churches. Debate was often harsh, but generally speaking the progress of what we now call the separation of church and state was considerable. Of course, a large part of the non-European world was at this time dominated, directly or indirectly, by European powers politically and by European values culturally. In much of Asia and the Middle East, there were strong forces calling for the cultural "modernization" of these areas. For some, this meant in practice the redefinition of religious values in a direction that was parallel to the dominant evolving theology of "liberal Protestantism" in the European zone. For others in the non-European zones, such as the socialist and Communist movements, it meant a non-religious, even anti-religious, framework for political activity.

This relegation of religion to something outside the political sphere reached its high point around the world in the period 1945-1970. This is something that can be seen clearly by looking at three major phenomena of this period. First, the definition of the central geopolitical issue was that of the so-called free world versus the Communist world. Though this had religious dimensions in that the Communist world was officially atheist and the "free world" attacked Communist systems for their constraints on religious institutions, still the debate was primarily formulated in terms of competing political philosophies, not competing religious faiths.

The second phenomenon is that those countries that defined themselves as "non-aligned" in the Cold War were for the most part dominated politically by movements of national liberation. These movements did not use religious affiliations as major categories of their discourse or their organizing. They were secular structures, and for the most part rather anticlerical, although this varied a bit according to local situations. In general, religiously defined political groups tended to be hostile to the governments established by the movements of national liberation or at least defined themselves as alternatives. Still such religiously defined movements did not command the support of the majority of the population in these countries.

The third phenomenon is the collapse of the resistance to the process of secularization of the state by its strongest religious opponent, the Roman Catholic Church. This is the heart of the political meaning of Pope John XXIII's *aggiornamento*, in which the Church accepted the idea that it was legitimate for the states to cut formal ties with religious institutions and operate in a context of religious pluralism. The Roman Catholic Church was now reduced to pleading for proportionate space in the public sphere, no longer daring to demand a monopoly.

To sum up this quick historical overview, we can say that there was a steady decline in the centrality of religious categories in the modern world-system from 1500 to *circa* 1970. Of course, one shouldn't exaggerate this. Religion still played a role, but often as little more than a marker of class affiliation. There is the famous definition of Great Britain's Established Church, the Church of England, as "the Tory party at prayer." Furthermore, it was well-recognized by both scholars and politicians in Great Britain that members of the so-called Dissenting Churches were much more likely to vote against the Tories—at first for the Liberals and later for Labor. And we could replicate this phenomenon of Church affiliation as a class category for much of the world.

It is quite clear nonetheless that the rise of so-called fundamentalisms throughout the world since *circa* 1970 represents a political shift of some importance. It reversed a five-century trend in the other direction. And we have to ask why this has happened and what are its political consequences.

THE WORLD-SYSTEM SINCE 1970

There are three fundamental changes in the world situation since the 1970s: the end of the Cold War; the collapse of the Old Left antisystemic movements; and stagnation in the world-economy which has led to profit-making primarily from financial speculation with a consequent sharp increase in the degree of polarization. Let me elaborate on each of these.

The end of the Cold War was a dramatic development about which everyone knows or thinks he knows. Institutionally, it meant the end of Communist regimes not only in east-central Europe but in the U.S.S.R. itself. It also meant the dismemberment of the three federal structures—the Soviet Union, Yugoslavia, and Czechoslovakia—into their constituent units (more or less). It meant the dissolution of the Warsaw Pact, and the entry of most east-central European states into NATO and into the European Union.

The end of the Cold War was generally hailed in the United States and western Europe as the political triumph of democracy over Communism, and Francis Fukuyama famously wrote about "the end of history." I have contended from the outset that the so-called victory of the U.S. and its allies was not a victory at all but rather a significant setback both for their geopolitical position and for their dominant values.[33]

The end of the Cold War served the geopolitical interests of the United States poorly for two main reasons. Despite the theoretical ideological struggle, or indeed perhaps because of it, the United States and the Soviet Union had been in tacit collusion throughout the Cold War, linked if by nothing else than by the fear of mutual destruction. This meant that the Soviet Union could and did use its political influence to constrain various countries of the South from upsetting the basic East-West geopolitical equilibrium, lest that lead to a nuclear war. The collapse of the Soviet Union meant the collapse of this kind of constraint mechanism. This had immediate consequences in the first Gulf war.

The second reason why the end of the Cold War was very undesirable from the point of view of the United States was that it eliminated totally the logic that underlay the close alliances of the United States with western Europe as well as with Japan and South Korea. These alliances had been based on common commitments to uniting in the Cold War against the Soviet Union. The alliances, having lost their *raison d'être*, risked coming unstrung. And, of course, we have seen in the second Gulf war how much unstringing there has in fact been.

The failures of the Old Left movements had their first major political consequence in the world revolution of 1968. In the post-1945 period, the Old Left movements had managed to come to power all around the globe—as Communist movements in the so-called socialist bloc; as social-democratic movements in the pan-European world; as national liberation movements in much of Asia, Africa, and the Caribbean; and as populist movements in much of Latin America.

They had come to power but they had manifestly not changed the world, which was the heart of the critique against them by the revolutionaries of 1968, who withdrew their confidence in these movements. They no longer believed in the ability of the Old Left movements to guarantee a better world for the future. Quite the contrary. They asserted that these movements in fact were sustaining the existing system. This reversal of attitude led on the one hand to the downfall in the following quarter of a century of many of the regimes these movements had put in place, and on the other hand to the emergence of a whole series of new kinds of movements that claimed they could replace the Old Left movements with movements following a different strategy, one that was less state-oriented and one that in fact would work better.

And finally, the capitalist world-economy, since *circa* 1970, has been in one long Kondratieff B-phase. Such B-phases are marked by several standard features: the increase worldwide in the unemployment rates and a generalized attack on wage levels; the shift of erstwhile leading industries that are no longer as profitable to semi-peripheral states (which thereupon assert that they are "developing"); the shift of capital from seeking profits via investment to seeking profits in the financial sphere; the attempt to reduce costs by attacking governmental pressures to internalize costs (in order to protect the environment) and by seeking to reduce taxation by reducing the protections of the welfare state. All of this has of course happened since the 1970s and is still going on.

We have been calling the conceptual discourse on behalf of these political efforts "neo-liberalism."

While some thin strata of the elite have gotten huge boosts of wealth from this kind of shift in emphasis in the world-economy, and a second slightly larger layer of the elite have done reasonably well in terms of current income, the overall situation is at least difficult economically, if not worse, for the large majority of the world's population. The principal political consequence is generalized fear about economic prospects, and hence a widespread search for protection, a restoration of some kind of safety net.

If we put these three elements together—end of the Cold War, disillusion with Old Left antisystemic movements, and stagnation in the world-economy—one can immediately see why political Islamism became a possible focus of the discourse. For the United States, it offered the image of a unifying enemy that might restore the overall alliance system in the absence of "communism" as a serious political force. For those who were deceived by the failures of the national liberation movements to ensure a better future (and indeed a reasonable present), political Islamism presented itself as a unifying alternative (especially in countries of largely Muslim populations), one that claimed it could achieve the presumed objectives of the national liberation movements far more efficaciously. And for all who were living amidst increased economic fears, it offered either a scapegoat or a symbol of hope, but in any case, it offered something concrete and different.

WHAT ARE "FUNDAMENTALISMS," AND WHERE?

In the last thirty years, we have seen everywhere the rise of so-called fundamentalisms—not only among Muslims, but among Christians, Jews, Hindus, and Buddhists. No doubt, the different religious versions have been located in different geographical zones, and each has its own historical roots and local variations. But the movements they have spawned in the last 30-35 years have some very obvious similarities.

The first is their complex relationship to state structures. On the one hand, all these movements assert that their legitimacy derives from instances more important than the state. They assert that the moral injunctions of their religious authorities and texts take priority over anything that states enact or ordain. In short, the laws of God (as these movements interpret them) overrule the taws of the state, which are merely the laws of human beings.

Yet, at the very same time that these movements assert such anti-secular, anti-state doctrines (and indeed act upon them quite flagrantly), they seek by every means conceivable to obtain state power. They say they do this in order that the state legislate the laws of God, and thereby impose them by the force of the state upon all who are disbelievers to any degree. And, of course, such groups have actually obtained state power in various places in recent years, and not only in the Islamic world. So we are able to see what are the consequences of this contradictory view of the state.

These movements play an ambiguous role vis-à-vis the state in still another way. They tend to assert that the states have failed in their obligations to provide basic social services to the mass of the population. This assertion is often largely correct. Feeling that it is futile to ask of corrupt state authorities to rectify this failure to do their duty as the religious movements conceive these duties, the various movements have tended to create substitute parastatal institutions. They create schools and dispensaries. They have their own equivalent of social workers to help individuals and families solve everyday problems, whether material, social, or psychological. They often have para-judicial institutions to deal with violations of moral norms, whether these are criminal or civil. In short, because the state has in their view failed to perform its duties properly, they seek to become the state *de facto* even when not yet *de jure*.

This assumption of a parastatal role has the double consequence of attracting a good deal of popular support from persons who have indeed been let down, or worse ignored, by the formal state apparatus. And of course, by performing these functions, they weaken, indeed delegitimize, the state structures still further.

It is often alleged that these so-called fundamentalist movements are anti-modern. This is quite incorrect. To be sure, their ideology tends to be formulated in terms of reviving moral rules that are claimed to be the truly traditional ones and are said to have been in operation in earlier times. Actually, this is usually only partially true. Some of these so-called traditional rules have been recent inventions. Others are enforced in ways more rigid than they were in earlier times. But even when the rules seem archaic in terms of modern value-systems (particularly in relation to rules about gender), they are in fact proposed as a way of dealing with present realities, or they are intended to fulfill secular objectives (such as the reinforcement of nationalism).

One of the things we can notice is that most of these movements are perfectly adept at the use of ultra-modern technologies, considering this absolutely legitimate, and attracting thereby the support of science and engineering students in their zones of concentration. These movements seldom endorse romantic returns to pre-modern life, unlike the Christian evangelical movements of the eighteenth century (such as the Amish) that still survive as isolated pockets among us. These movements should be thought of therefore as alternative forms of modernism. They are not only modernist but they are aggressively proselytizing. They seek for the most part to impose their particular version of modernism on the entire world, and particularly on all those living within the states within which they are operating.

WHY SINGLE OUT ISLAM?

If these movements exist in almost all areas of the world, with very comparable agendas, why is it that so much attention is paid to Islamism? No other form of politicized, "fundamentalist" religious movements get comparable notice, except perhaps the so-called Christian Right whose base is in evangelical Christian churches. These two sets of religious movements form a pair. In Sri Lanka, for example, the Tamil movement is secular but its adherents are largely Hindu. They are fighting against a government whose power base is among Buddhists. The Tamil Tigers more or less invented the idea of suicide bombers, and are still using it extensively. Yet almost everyone associates suicide bombing with Islam and Islamists, not with secular Hindus. So something else is going on here.

One reason is the obvious one. Political Islamists have identified the United States as the guiding evil force in the world, and have taken to attacking the United States openly and directly. They have also of course been attacking Muslims, and especially Muslim regimes and rulers, whom they believe to be heretical and acting in collusion with the United States. We even have shorthand to allude to this phenomenon: it is 9/11.

It is also obvious how the image of a large and continuing threat from those designated as "Islamic terrorists" has served the political interests of the Bush regime as well. This explains why it has done everything it could to enracinate this concept in the popular consciousness. "Terrorism" is an inherently blurry concept, and it is therefore loosely applied, often beyond anyone's desires and expectations. In a chaotic geopolitical arena, such blurry but powerful concepts are hard to deal with, even harder to eradicate, and still harder to contain.

Since Muslims are now spread throughout the globe more or less, and since in many areas Muslims are part of oppressed minorities, Islamist extremism becomes a theme that various local power structures in turn find useful to justify their politics of repression, and to seek thereupon political support from the United States and other pan-European powers. A rolling stone thereby begins to gather quite a bit of moss.

It is then possible to call upon memories of historical conflicts that had been long buried: the Crusades and the long and successful resistance by Muslims to the twelfth-century Christian occupation of Palestine. It is not really that there are very many people today who want literally to revive the Crusades, it is rather that this reference serves as a dim legitimation of present-day sentiments.

This is in fact where Israel conies in. Whatever the attitudes and motives of Israelis and of Jews elsewhere in the world, it is clear that Israel's existence and policies are a major bone of contention between large numbers of those who are Muslims (however nominal) and those who are Christian (however nominal). On both sides, there has come to be an explicit Christian-Jewish combine in political terms which, when one thinks about it, is truly remarkable, considering how recent were the terrible consequences of historic Christian anti-Semitism for Jews. But politics, as always, makes strange bedfellows.

Then there is the great utility for states with a largely Muslim population to emphasize the Islamic character as a mode of national identification and reinforcement. The most secular of movements finds it hard to avoid. I give two instances. In 1955, Algerian students in France organized the *Union Générate des Etudiants Musulmans Algériens* (or UGEMA). Considering the fact that UGEMA was formed by the Front de Liberation National (FLN), a very secular liberation movement, and considering that the overwhelming majority of Algerian students in France were quite secular, why did they put the word *musulmans* in their name? The answer is quite simple. It was to distinguish them from the previously existing *Union Générate des Etudiants Algériens* (UGEA), which had Muslim, Christian, and Jewish members, and most importantly which was opposed to the idea of Algerian independence. By referring to Islam, UGEMA was proclaiming its nationalism.

I give a second example. The *Ba'ath* party was in its origins and practice a very secular, radical pan-Arab movement. Its founder was in fact a Christian. It eventually came to power in both Syria and Iraq, and Saddam Hussein, as we know, was a Ba'athist. His regime was not only secular but extremely unfriendly to Islamist groups. Yet, after the first Gulf War, Saddam Hussein began to assume some Islamic clothing, albeit somewhat lightly. It was a way for him to try to reinforce Iraqi nationalism and reduce internal opposition to his policies.

So, there we are today. We live in a world with multiple violences committed in the name of constructed cultural oppositions between a reified Islamism and a reified pan-Europeanism (which scarcely hides its Christian character). As long as the political conflicts persist, such concepts are self-reinforcing and self-perpetuating. Rational analysis has little impact on their hold on popular imaginations. The question is simply, how long can they last, since for the most part they are built on straw. What is going on in the world today is much more than a debate about religious values and institutions.

THE LEFT AND POLITICAL ISLAMISM

The world Left has not known how to handle the rise of religious "fundamentalisms." Specifically, they have been totally unsure whether, as some suggest, they should hail their emergence as a new variety of antisystemic movement or, at the other extreme, consider that they are a major enemy of left movements and values and should be thought of as a new variety of fascist-like movements. For the most part, most left movements have responded by saying very little and relegating themselves to observing the political consequences of the rise of such movements.

There is good reason for such ambiguity. On the one hand, the world Left is heir to movements which more or less felt, as Marx did, that religion is the opiate of the masses. Of course, there have always been leftists who espoused religious values, but it is also true that they represented a minority within the ranks of the world Left and were at most tolerated by the others. So it is natural that the contemporary world political Left throws a somewhat skeptical eye, if not a frankly hostile one, on religiously based "fundamentalist" political movements.

On the other hand, the world Left often finds that such movements are fighting the same enemies that it is fighting. Most specifically, the world Left and most "fundamentalist" movements (but especially the Islamist ones) consider the United States (both in general and in its Bush regime version in particular) as the primary structure upholding the existing world-system and therefore the primary force to oppose. The old political wisdom is that the enemy of my enemy is my friend.

If one looks at the primary meeting-ground of the world Left today, the World Social Forum (WSF), one will immediately observe several things. While some religiously-based movements attend and even play an important role (for example, the left Christian movements in Brazil), no "fundamentalist" movement of any religious persuasion is there. The second thing to notice is that neither "fundamentalism" in general nor political Islamism in particular seems to be at all on the agenda for debate. In a forum that discusses virtually everything, the absence of such debate is striking. Even when one of its major meetings took place in a Muslim country—the meeting in Karachi in March 2006—this issue did not seem to have been on the agenda.

Of course, for the world Left, religious "fundamentalism" is not the only thorny issue. There is the issue of the role to be allotted intellectually and politically to "ethnicist" or "indigenist" movements. But unlike the "fundamentalist" movements, "ethnicist" or "indigenist" movements have not only been active in the World Social Forum, but many active persons have been seeking their even greater participation.

To be sure, there is some debate about the attitude that should be taken towards them. There have been critics from a sort of traditional Old Left view who have argued that "ethnicist" or "indigenist" movements are divisive of the Left and unreliable in the long run because they refuse to recognize the centrality of class issues. But at least the matter is debated, indeed debated loudly and with passion, but debated also intelligently as a question of basic Left strategy in the twenty-first century world.

One might have thought that the WSF would have had the same kind of debate about the "fundamentalist" movements. To be sure, most of these movements have been politically on the right. This is certainly true of the principal Christian, Jewish, Hindu, and Buddhist movements. The only noteworthy examples of those that are not unambiguously on the right are indeed the Islamist movements. But they are certainly not unambiguously on the left either.

Are we perhaps discussing this matter too early? As these Islamist movements begin to assume state power in more and more states, will they be coming into more direct conflict with secular Left movements? This happened in Iran and to some extent in Sudan and Yemen. It may be happening in post-Saddam Iraq. In Algeria, Left movements generally tended to sympathize with the non-Left government's crackdown on Islamist movements. Everywhere, the secular Left, such as it is in largely Muslim countries, is caught between its unhappiness with the regimes in power and its fears about what would happen— to them—if Islamist movements came to power. Consequently, they have been politically paralyzed.

THE COMING DECADES

It is no doubt far too early to say the religious "fundamentalist" movements have passed their prime and are beginning to decline as central political forces in their countries. But it does seem to me likely that this point will come, and perhaps sooner than we think. For example, there are some signs that some evangelical Christians in the United States are beginning to rethink their active participation in Republican party politics and are considering a possible return to their traditional attitude of distancing themselves from the political scene. When the Bharatiya Janata Party (BJP) came to power in India, they found that their commitment to Hindu "fundamentalist" politics was a hindrance to their staying in power, and they clearly moderated their views.

In Iran, popular pressure seemed to have forced the regime, over the past twenty-five years, to allow a creeping liberalization of mores in order to remain on top of the situation. Furthermore, the current central emphasis of the Iranian regime is not on Islamist values but on the rights of Iran to a full development of nuclear energy. This position has been extremely popular in Iran and has certainly reinforced the hold of the regime on power. But nuclear energy is a secular, nationalist theme, not an Islamist one. Does this not represent a quiet shift in ideology, and will this not have longer-run consequences internally for Iran?

No doubt, we may expect a weakening of the "fundamentalist" character of religiously based movements precisely as a result of their successes in achieving state power. Nuclear energy or its equivalent will take pride of place over *sharia* or anti-abortion or their equivalents. We have seen how much the achievement of state power gutted the commitments of Old Left antisystemic movements to their traditional ideologies and political promises. Why should this not be the same with "fundamentalist" movements when they come to state power?

The real question is not what will happen to these movements as a result of their successes in the coming decades. The real question is what will happen to the world Left and to their present major incarnation, the World Social Forum, in the coming decades. The WSF, after just a few years of existence in which it grew steadily and became a relative political success, is now facing a turning-point.

There has long been a tension, now more acute, between two large groups. There are those who emphasized the role of the WSF as an "open space," one that was "horizontal" as opposed to the hierarchical structures of the various historic internationals. And there are those who think the WSF must become a locus of concerted political action on the world level.

The logic of each side is clear. To emphasize horizontally and open space is to opt for a vast coalition of groups of very different kinds and projects, whose sole unifying requirement is a commitment by any and all participants that they are opposed to neo-liberalism and to imperialism in all its forms. To ensure the breadth of the coalition, the WSF has no officers and passes no resolutions. It is simply a forum in which different groups of activists may exchange views and increase their practical collaboration outside the WSF framework.

For the others, the horizontal structure reduces the WSF to being a "talking shop," which is boring and ultimately politically irrelevant. The WSF must, they say, organize worldwide political activities. The first group answers that this formula would lead rapidly to exclusions of those who had different views and reduce the WSF to repeating the failures of the previous internationals. Unless the WSF can overcome this division with some formula that is possible for both camps to accept, it will disintegrate.

The merit of the open forum formula is obvious. It allows one to create a very large coalition of every movement composed of left-leaning people and takes positions that are somehow "left of center"—from the most moderate to the most radical. Indeed, the only question one might raise about such a concept is that of the few exclusions the WSF practices—that of political parties, that of movements which engage in military action, and implicitly that of the "fundamentalist" religious movements. I myself would open it to all of these, provided only that they are committed to the minimal ideological cement of the WSF—opposition to neoliberalism and to imperialism in all its forms. Since the open forum formula allows for no voting, no officers, no agreed-upon resolutions, there is little risk that including these groups in the forum would lead to some kind of "takeover" by them, thereby changing the character of the WSF.

On the other hand, it is clear that world political activity is an essential element of transforming the world in this period of systemic transition in which we are living. And the WSF as an open forum is not constructed to engage in such directly militant activity. So I would favor the creation of multiple ad hoc coalitions of groups that were ready to engage in specific political campaigns, and consider that these are outgrowths of WSF's open space. They would not be endorsed as such by the collectivity of those present, but only speak for such movements and individuals who indicated their adherence to a particular political campaign.

It will only be in the intellectual and political give and take of the unlimited discussions at the open space and the multiple ad hoc political activities that will be created that we can hope to achieve that combination of united front and meaningful political activity that would give the world Left the possibility of bringing into being that "other world that is possible."

And it will be this road to lucidity and political effectiveness that will enable us to relegate religious credos and passions to their appropriate place in the public political sphere, and set us once again on the path to both a greater democratic participation by everyone and a more egalitarian world political, economic, and social structure. If this happens, in 2050, we shall look back to the period 1970 to perhaps 2020 at most as an interesting interlude and not at all as the face of the future.

III

PERSPECTIVES OF AFRICAN THINKERS

9

A COMMENT ON EPISTEMOLOGY: WHAT IS AFRICA?

In the beginning were the words, and the words were with the gods, and the words were the gods. There were many peoples and each had its gods. This is still true, except that the "Western" religious tradition developed an important variation on the theme. First, the multiplicity of gods was replaced in this tradition by a singular god, who thereupon had to be the god of all the world. The only version still extant of this first phase of the shift to monotheism is Judaism. Judaism managed to combine the idea of one god for all with the idea of a "chosen people." This combination restrained the universalism of Jewish monotheism, but it also restrained the intrusiveness.

Jewish monotheism was succeeded by two other versions, Christianity and Islam, which eliminated the "chosen people" idea. However, the logic of this elimination was that there was no longer any restraint on universalist claims. This meant inevitably that these religions had to become proselytizing religions. Both did in fact proselytize, with some considerable success in each case, but of course less than total success. The African continent's religious pattern in the twentieth century is good evidence of this relative but not total success. As we know, the emergence of the capitalist world-economy, originally located in a Christian zone of the world, was accompanied by a process of "secularization." In this process, Christian proselytization for its universal god was to some extent replaced by, to some extent overlain by, a more secular form of universalism, incarnated in the concepts of scientific truth and technological progress. Marxism derived from this latter tradition and was one major variant of this assertion of the reality of universal truth.

The African continent was thus confronted in the process of its incorporation into the capitalist world-economy by an intrusive ideology which not only rejected the worth of the gods who had been Africa's but also was pervasive in that it took on multiple clothings: Christianity, science, democracy, Marxism. This experience was not of course unique to the African continent, nor was the reaction of Africa unique. Cultural resistance everywhere to this intrusive, insistent, newly dominant ideology took ambiguous forms. On the one hand, many Africans accepted, seemed to accept, the new universalism, seeking to learn its secrets, seeking to tame this god, seeking to gain its favor. On the other hand, many Africans (often the same ones) rebelled against it. There is nothing surprising in this. It has long been commonplace to observe such an ambiguous reaction. The situation is such that we can speak of a double bind, in which there was no reaction that could remove the pressure and the oppression.

In the course of the last one hundred years, the concept of Africa has emerged. It is a European word, and its definition was first given by Europeans. But those so defined have struggled in recent years to take control of the defining process, or to take more control of this process, which is inherently a process that is both continuous and always reciprocal (that is, never one-sided). For example, the political decision taken in 1958 at the first Conference of Independent African States in Accra states "north of the Sahara" within the definition of Africa has had important and thus far lasting effects.

Nonetheless, as long as we live in a singular, hierarchical world-system, the capitalist world-economy, posing the question of whether a set of ideas, or a way of thinking, is universal (European) or African returns us only to the double bind which the system itself has created. If we are to get out of this double bind, we must take advantage of the contradictions of the system itself to go beyond it.

We must start with the classic question of Jean Genét in *Les nègres* (Décines: Marc Barbezat, 1960). "Mais, qu'est-ce que c'est donc un noir? et d'abord, c'est de quelle couleur?" What Genet is trying to make us realize is that the definition of the universal is a particular definition of a particular system—the modern world-system—and that, within that system, the definition of the particular has no particularities but is a universal of that system. As long as that system is functioning reasonably well, the debate about the relationship of the universal and the particular is not only vain and unresolvable but also the very process of the debate tends to reinforce the structure of cultural hierarchy and oppression internal to that system.

It is only when the system itself comes into systemic crisis that, at the level of idea-systems as well as at that of social movements, we have real options and therefore the possibility of real debates. But we are in such a systemic crisis now. And we are in such a debate. However, it is well to be clear what the debate is about. It is not about whether there is, has been, or could be a "specifically African" set of ideas or concepts or worldviews that could substitute for, supplement, or rebut a Western set, either in the study of Africa or of anything else. To pose the question that way is to place us back into the double bind, to play the game in terms of the rules of an oppressive system now in crisis.

The debate is rather about two things. What is science, and what is scientific knowledge? Not in Africa, but everywhere. It is a question as much for North America or Western Europe as for Africa. The second question is what systemic options do we have. If the modern world-system is in crisis, what alternatives present themselves? If it were true that "progress" is inevitable, then the question would be meaningless. But if rather we accept that systemic transitions can go in various directions, then and only then do we have an epistemological question: how can we know the range of options, and what kinds of scientific endeavors will further one or another option?

The contribution of Africans (I am not sure if one can call it the contribution of Africa) could be that the weight and constraints of the existing idea-systems tend to rest less heavily on them than on Europeans, and the movements that emerge there—in the larger political arena, and in the academy—will hopefully reflect this. It may be therefore that more coherent insights into options will arise there. But they will only arise if they are not placed in the old cul-de-sac of universalism versus particularism.

10

THE EVOLVING ROLE OF THE AFRICA SCHOLAR IN AFRICAN STUDIES

This paper was originally written for a panel on the major paradigms dealing with change in Africa. But I wish to deal less with the evolution of so-called paradigms than with evolution of the role of the specialized student of change in Africa. One cannot dissociate the two, and I do not intend to do so. But in discussions on theorizing, there occurs too often a neglect of the theorizers, which in turn may lead to misinterpretations of what is and was going on.

As we all know, before *circa* 1950 the study of Africa was confined very largely to the domain of anthropology. True, there were some partial exceptions. In the case of South Africa, the large white population and the relative importance of its participation in the world-economy meant that some economists studied it as well. And in the case of North Africa, what might be called "Islamics" also played a role.

Nonetheless, anthropology dominated the scene. The fact that the study of Africa was thus limited of course reflected the division of intellectual labor that had been carved out in the late nineteenth century, among whose features was the division of the world into three geographical zones: modern European and European-settler states, which were studied by economists, historians, political scientists, and sociologists; non-Western areas with a long-standing written culture and preferable a so-called "world religion," which were studied by so-called Orientalists; and backward peoples, which were studied by anthropologists.

Furthermore, the anthropology of which we are speaking, and which emerged as a serious corpus of work between the two World Wars, was strongly anti-historical in orientation. It centered on two concepts. One was the existence of some original pattern of social behavior of some entity usually designated a "tribe" which was thought to be internally unchanging and whose processes, in the "post-contact" situation that had caused change, had to be recaptured by careful field work. Once recaptured, these processes were described in the famous "ethnographic present." The second concept was precisely that of "cultural contact" or "acculturation." At some point, it was said, the unchanging traditional entity had come into "contact" with some outside force and changes had occurred in the "culture." These changes, too, could be studied by contemporary observation. This was considered more "applied" research than that of recapturing the "disappearing culture."

Behind these two concepts lay a rather strong ideological bias: that the "cultures" of these "tribes," *even if they were not Western cultures*, were still legitimate objects of study. There were two different explanations for this view. One was based on the premise of evolution. Since all peoples pass through identical (or at least very similar) stages, tribal cultures were merely located somewhere on a continuum. They were further back to be sure than European cultures, but this in itself made them of interest. The alternative explanation was that of cultural relativism. Since all cultures represented equally worthy solutions for the basic human problems of adaptation to the environment, what seemed strange would seem less so, once the anthropologist uncovered the code and translated it into Western terminology.

Who were these anthropologists? They were almost all either university-trained scholars on the one hand or colonial administrators or missionaries (with a scholarly bent) on the other. By and large, they all did field work in the same basic way. They lived in a given area for some time, learned the local language more or less, and utilized indigenous assistants as informants, intermediaries, and companions.

These anthropologists were all Europeans, and almost always of the nationality of the governing colonial power. The precondition for their work was indeed the fact that these "tribes" were located in areas governed by colonial authorities. But the precondition was also a major constraint. Anthropologists needed the permission of the colonial authorities to do their work. Of course, they also needed the permission of the "tribe" to do their work. The first permission was indispensable and formal. The second was only necessary in the sense that it was believed such permission, the culmination of an effort to achieve "rapport," was required for the work to be "successful."

Once such rapport was achieved, it was generally considered intruding for other anthropologists to invade the same terrain. Each anthropologist had his "tribe" and there were after all enough to go around.

When the work was completed, it took the form of a monograph or a report. Its audience was other anthropologists in the Western world (but first of all in the particular metropole) and all those involved at a high level in administrative work in the colonies. The research yielded some empirical knowledge of very practical use to administrators, some additional evidence of ethnographic variation for use by scholars, and very occasionally some insight into theoretical propositions.

In political terms, the anthropologists of this period were essentially secular missionaries, liberal mediators between the tribe and the Colonial Office (plus metropolitan public opinion). The anthropologists were concerned (a) to demonstrate that "backward" did not necessarily mean "primitive" or "irrational," and (b) to ensure that the negative social consequences of "contact" be minimized and the positive ones maximized.

Anthropologists thought of themselves as sympathetic "strangers" in both cultures. To the African "tribe," they came as "strangers" who however engaged in "participant observation," and therefore combined subjective empathy with objective perspective. (This was incidentally the same stance which historians at the time used to justify their choice of double practical constraints: a lifetime specialization on a limited space-time zone which was thought to create subjective empathy, and the choice of such a zone at a distant time, thought to ensure an objective perspective.) The anthropologist however also considered himself a stranger to metropolitan culture. Indeed, the psychological roots of choosing anthropology as a career was often, as we know, a sense of partial alienation from one's own culture. The anthropologist felt that he was unlike his fellow metropolitans, in that he was exempt from "ethnocentrism" (just as the missionary felt unlike laymen in that he was exempt from "materialism" or "secularism"). There was no doubt an element of self-congratulation in this stance.

The changes that began *circa* 1950 were not the doing of the Africa scholars. They were the consequence of the rise of African nationalism in the form of political movements. Nationalist movements by their very existence challenged, both implicitly and explicitly, the two basic premises of the previous work of Africa scholars.

First, nationalist movements asserted that the primary arena of social and political action, in terms of legitimacy and hence of study, was and ought to be the colonial state/putative nation, and not the "tribe." Indeed, they went further. They argued that emphasis on "tribes" and "tribalism" was a central device of the colonial authorities to maintain the colonial rule, and as a consequence they formally deplored the study of "tribes."

Secondly, nationalist movements asserted that the relationship between Europeans and Africans had not been one of "culture contact" at all, but rather one of a "colonial situation." Culture contact could be good or bad and, as we have just noted, the anthropologists had devoted themselves politically to trying to make sure it was good rather than bad. Colonial situations could only be bad. The only thing one could do to achieve good in a colonial situation was to end it. The primary force to ensure that culture contact would be good rather than bad had been the "liberal mediator." The primary force to ensure that the colonial situation would be ended had to be an African nationalist movement. Politically, therefore the nationalist movements were advocating "African agency" in place of "European agency."

The anthropologists, of the genre that had flourished in the interwar period, were deprived of the legitimacy of their subject matter. Some drew drastic conclusions. Georges Balandier, trained as an anthropologist, invented the term "colonial situation," and became a professor of sociology at the Sorbonne.

In a world that was decolonizing, African studies became drastically redefined. African colonies-becoming-independent-states now seemed to exhibit political, economic, and social processes sufficiently similar to those of the West such that they could be seen as the normal domain of political scientists, economists, and sociologists. Africa prior to colonial rule no longer seemed some unchanging entity, but could be seen as the normal domain of historians and archaeologists. African culture no longer seemed an exoticism but could be seen as the normal domain of students of literature or art or film or music. In short, all of a sudden and quite rapidly, everyone got into the act.

There was concurrently a drastic shift in the social composition of Africa scholars. A field that previously had been composed almost exclusively of citizens of the European colonial powers was now transformed by two massive new groups. Scholars in the United States, who prior to 1945, had virtually been one man—Melville Herskovits—now began to invade every remote corner of the continent. Among these American scholars, there was an important contingent of Black American scholars. The growth of the African Studies Association (ASA) itself, from the 35 or so people who founded it in 1957 to the jamboree of 1982, attests to this phenomenon dramatically. This growth was not accidental or unplanned. It was nurtured, encouraged, and financed by the great private foundations and the U.S. government. It was the inevitable outcome of the strong political interests which the United States, as the world's new hegemonic power, had assumed after the Second World War.

There was a second massive new group of Africa scholars: the Africans. Before 1945, there had been virtually only one—Jomo Kenyatta—and how extraordinary that had seemed at the time. Now there were many Africans, trained at universities, initially in the West and later in Africa itself. For, along with the rise of African Africa scholars went the rise of the African universities. The emergence of these African Africa scholars was directly linked to the rise of the nationalist movements, not because these scholars were political activists (of course some were) but because it was the existence of these movements that created the social conditions for the educational structures that sustained the African Africa scholars.

There were of course others who became Africa scholars in this period—in the U.S.S.R., in non-colonizing European countries, in Canada and Australia, in India and Japan, and in Brazil. In short, when we say that everybody got into the act, we mean not only the range of university-recognized disciplines but the geographical range of world scholarship.

The basic premises of the new collective work were, in dialectical response to the earlier scholarship, the inverse of the previous premises. The state/nation was now the locus of social action, and African agency provided the dynamic focus of the analysis. For a while, the center of much analysis was on such phenomena as the nationalist movements, state-building (both pre-colonial and post-colonial), so-called primary resistance, and Negritude.

Despite this massive social restructuring of the personnel engaging in Africa studies, their basic political stance in the period 1950-1970 was not as different from that of the pre-1950 anthropologists as one might have expected. I have suggested that the pre-1950 anthropologists could be seen as "liberal mediators" and "secular missionaries." In various ways, the 1950-1970 Africa scholars continued to act in these roles.

Prior to 1950, Africa scholars mediated between their tribe and the colonial administrator. The new 1950-1970 brand of Africa scholars mediated between modern Africa (represented first of all by the nationalist movements) and the Western world in general. But mediation now took the form not of interpreting "traditional African customs and values" but of interpreting "modern African behavior." The Africa scholars sought to interpret this behavior first of all to Western policy-makers at all levels, in order to make them more "sympathetic" to the positions argued by the modern African leaders. And they sought to interpret African behavior to the vast majority of scholars concerned primarily with the West, in order to make them reformulate their generalizations to take into account some of the specificities of the African situation.

Performing this role of mediating interpretation, Africa scholars still were self-congratulatory about the fact that they were thereby overcoming "ethnocentrism." The scholars in the United states assumed this role of "liberal mediation" with even greater enthusiasm than did their European or Soviet colleagues, who however in fact did the same, as did even the African Africa scholars.

But if the Africa scholars continued to be "liberal mediators," did they also continue to be "secular missionaries?" Of course they did. The very same Africa scholars who engaged in the interpretive political tasks turned right around and assigned themselves the role of counselor and advisor to African institutions, overtly and covertly, explicitly and implicitly, invited or uninvited. And they played this role with the best of conscience, pursuing their appointed tasks in the spread of rationality and progress as decreed by the Enlightenment and transmitted via science and scholarship.

The 1969 meeting of the African Studies Association (U.S.) thus came as an earthquake to Africa scholars, first of all in the United States but not only in that country. The meetings were held in the wake of the student and worker rebellions that had been occurring in many parts of the world since 1968. In the United States, a major component of the political turmoil had been the expression of the Black Power movement. The meetings were in Montreal. This meant that, exceptionally, the meetings had a very large non-United States contingent. First of all, the ASA was meeting jointly with our Canadian sister body. Secondly, since it was the first such joint meeting, and since it was taking place in the province of Quebec (itself going through parallel political turmoil), the Canadians had raised money to invite many European and African scholars—from both the Anglophone and Francophone scholarly networks.

We were assembled for the grand opening when a group of Black American Africa scholars seized the platform and put forward a series of demands. These demands had not come out of the blue. There had been signs of discontent for two years previously, including the founding of a Black American grouping of Africa scholars known as the African Heritage Studies Association (AHSA). The political dynamics of the Montreal meeting were complex, and it is not to the point to review them. What is to the point is to see the nature of the demands that were being made.

There were two major complaints, and both revolved around the social role of the Africa scholar. One was the complaint that Africa studies in the United States were built on a foundation of institutional racism, which protected the control of the field by white Establishment scholars located in the major universities. For example, it was argued, there had been virtually no Blacks who were in leadership positions of the ASA, or who were the recipients of major grants by funding agencies. A number of solutions were proposed: opening up ASA membership to non-university persons concerned with Africa, and racial parity on the Executive Council of ASA were among them.

The second complaint concerned what I have called the stance of "liberal mediator." The charge was made that it reflected in some cases hypocrisy and in others inefficacity. This was the period of the unmasking of the CIA's covert involvement in non-governmental organizations, including some associated with Africa studies, such as AMSAC (the American Society of African Culture) and the AAI (African-American Institute). This was also the period when the whole concept of academic non-involvement in overtly political debates was being widely called into question. A number of solutions were proposed: among them were the formal rejection of the legitimacy of links of Africa scholars not only to the CIA but to all other United States governmental agencies as well (State Department, AID, USIA, etc.); and open political support for liberation movements in Africa as well as for progressive governments.

The world of Africa scholarship was deeply split and emotionally wrenched by the confrontation. As an immediate outcome, a great many (perhaps most) Black American Africa scholars withdrew from the ASA, and AHSA transformed itself from being a supplementary structure of United States-based Africa scholars to being a rival organization.

In the following five years, the inter-organizational tension calmed down, but the rift has never been fully healed. Eventually, the ASA responded to the crisis by certain organizational changes: some democratization of membership categories; election of Blacks to leadership positions; the creation of the Committee on Current Issues to permit the regular public airing of Africa-related political issues; adoption of resolutions on political questions. In 1973, the ASA agreed to create a joint delegation with AHSA on a basis of parity to attend the International Congress of Africanists, and agreed to support John Henrik Clarke of AHSA as the sole United States candidate for the Executive Council of the international organization.

That body itself made a symbolic shift of some importance in 1973. It changed its name. It had been known, since its founding in 1962, as the International Congress of Africanists. After deliberation, the group decided that "Africanist" was a label redolent of the outsider looking in (which historically was true, since the term was an emendation of Orientalist), and hence from then on the organization was to be called the International Congress of African Studies.

In the 1970s thus the Africa scholar's social role of "liberal mediator" began to wither away, and there were many individuals who withdrew from the field as a consequence. I would argue this was also one reason for the decline of student interest in Africa studies, though not the only one to be sure.

Meanwhile, much was happening on other fronts besides merely Africa studies. The crisis in developmentalist ideology—of both the liberal and Marxist variety—had led to the reopening of the epistemological and historiographical bases of modern social science. This is not the place to review that subject, but the fact of this happening is central to our story.

In Africa, as a political arena, the "downward sweep of African liberation" which had gone into a long pause in 1965 was resumed dramatically in 1974. By now African nationalist movements had been superseded by national liberation movements, and this represented more than a mere semantic shift. African Marxisms (my plural is deliberate) emerged on the scene as a major factor for the first time—on the political scene, and on the intellectual scene. And the central locus of Africa studies was shifting from the trinity United States-United Kingdom-France to the African continent.

I have drawn a picture in broad brush strokes. Still I think it is accurate, if not complete. What are its implications for the present? We are in the midst of these changes. It is by no means certain where they will end. The social composition of African scholarship in the 1990s, the ideological premises, and above all the social role of the Africa scholar will be determined by the confluence of transformations in the world-system as a whole (including world scholarship) and the political struggles on the African continent.

The schism of 1969 may, indeed probably will, reappear in an updated and more radicalized form—one in which the veneer will be less race than class. What is sure is that we are being called upon to make renewed fundamental choices in terms of the analytic frameworks we are able and willing to employ, and the values we are able and ready to uphold. In that sense, we are very far from the beginnings of Africa studies, when we rationalized the analysis of exotica. Africa studies is now as central to world scholarship as any other subfield. Indeed, the question is, in what meaningful sense is there today a subfield we can call Africa studies?

11

BASIL DAVIDSON'S AFRICAN ODYSSEY

When I was younger and trying to discover Africa, Basil Davidson wrote a book entitled *The Lost Cities of Africa* whose introduction was entitled "The Rediscovery of Africa." The whole point was there. It was a salutary, fundamental point which may seem very banal today, but in 1959 not only was it not banal, it was controversial. And therein, as they say, lies a tale.

I've never been wholly clear how it was that Basil Davidson first came to discover, then to rediscover Africa. During the second world war he was busily engaged working with resistance movements in southeastern and southern Europe, most notably with the Partisans in Yugoslavia and Italy. He served as a British liaison officer, and soon found that the only useful way to pursue his task of achieving a common goal, the defeat of the Nazis, was to catapult his role into being a Partisan liaison officer with the British It is a lesson he carried over to Africa.

He is, of course, a man of passion as well as intelligence, and he has never hidden the fact that his heart is on the left for more freedom and more equality, not less; and for more now, and not later. He was not the only European of such persuasion to have become attracted to Africa's struggles in the postwar era. But he followed a different path from most of these. Many came as activist advisers to movements seeking to reclaim African control over their destinies.

They no doubt played a helpful role, but in the very nature of the movements they were aiding, such a role could only be at best a temporary and precarious one. And so it proved to be in instance after instance.

Others came not as advisers but as students of current developments. And this too was, and remains, very important, but it too has its risks, for a European scholarly student of the African present risks being caught up in the subtle institutional web of European policy concerns. Basil Davidson has of course written about the present. He has been a remarkable analyst of the national liberation movements in formerly Portuguese Africa, for one thing. And we owe him a deep debt for that, for without him we would have been notably less well informed during the crucial years of the liberation wars in this zone of Africa. And he certainly resisted those subtle institutional webs.

Nonetheless, I do not count those books as his major contribution. For me, his contribution has been to the rediscovery of Africa, to the process of overcoming the West's shameful ignorance of the history of the world. He was one of the few who early on decided to devote themselves to recreating a coherent narrative interpretation of the sweep of African history. He did not work alone. He was inspired for example by Gervase Matthew and Thomas Hodgkin, to whom he dedicated *Lost Cities*. But seen over thirty years of work, his corpus of work is probably unmatched in its scope and in its wide-ranging influence.

Let us start by underlining what he did not do. He did not instruct Africans how to reinterpret their past. There is a marvelous reserve in how he has written. Rather, he listened very carefully, seeking to discover how African historians—the Ajayis, the Boahens, the Ki Zerbos, the Ogots, the Cheikh Anta Diops—were doing this. And not only the African historians, but the African social thinkers, the African novelists and the African street intellectuals. All the while, he travelled and read voraciously in and about Africa.

And then he recounted it to us in a rich, textured manner. I see that on the jacket of *Let Freedom Come: Africa in Modern History* (published in 1978). There is a blurb from the *New York Review of Books* which praises Basil Davidson as "the most effective popularizer of African history and archaeology outside Africa, and certainly the one best trusted in Black Africa itself." Often in the world of academia, the term "popularizer" is the supreme put-down. Basil Davidson is a popularizer, if by that we mean someone who writes (and writes well and writes consciously) for a wider audience than other scholars. He is much more than that, but he is that.

But, think of what he has been popularizing and where. He has not been evoking Joan of Arc for the French, or even Marco Polo's voyages to exotic Cathay for Renaissance Italy. He has been telling twentieth-century Western audiences that Africa has had a complex, exciting history for thousands of years—a "long, continuous, and broadly definable movement."[34] He has been demonstrating that Africans have brought a great deal to Senghor's "rendez-vous du dormer et du recevoir." If he has popularized that, this is no mean feat.

For that is the point. When he began to write, we were all still immersed in the aberrant but deeply-ensconced cultural ambiance of European colonialism. Racism did not even have to be hidden, except in the most polite circles. And H. R. Trevor-Roper was opining that there was no such thing as African history since if there were no writing (not even true!), there was no history. In the 1950s the very subject matter still found no place in Western universities—and hardly in African for that matter since African universities were just beginning to emerge from the heavy tutelary hand of the metropoles. To write the *Lost Cities of Africa* in 1959 was breathtaking. It certainly changed my view of the world, and I cannot believe that this was not its effect on many, many others.

I am not suggesting that Basil Davidson singlehandedly transformed the general attitudes in the West about Africa from scorn to admiration. For one thing, it is extremely doubtful that the transformation has been as profound as that. For another, the political reality of Africa's movements has done more to force mental reassessments than anyone's writings. Still, things have changed. And where Basil Davidson did play a great role was to get us, or at least many of us, to take African history seriously.

The question is, does this matter? And to whom? First of all, of course it matters to Africans. African history is such an incredibly serious business these days, with hundreds of really first-rate scholars—African and non-African—working on it that one must marvel at its progress as a locus of scholarly research. The UNESCO *General History of Africa*, a splendid interim synthesis itself only in process, is testimony to how much has been learned.

And this knowledge has made a big difference to contemporary Africa. No doubt that is a bit difficult to demonstrate, for it is hard to point to many real policy decisions that have been made in function of new historical knowledge. And yet this is not the crucial test. The crucial test is whether the current generation of Africans in their 20s, and those to come in the next 30-50 years, suffer from what Sekou Toure called the "complex of the colonized" to the degree that young Africans did in, say, the 1950s. The complex of the colonized is not an easy malformation to correct but I have no doubt that some significant progress has been made. In this correction, the rediscovery of African history has played no small role. It is an arduous task to reconvert mentalities, but it is not Sisyphean.

The energy devoted thereto is not ill-spent. Reconverting African mentalities, and thereby reaching the point where Africans take full control of their own destinies by taking control of their own minds, is a crucial anti-imperialist goal and, as I've said, one that is on its way to being realized. In this odyssey, Basil Davidson has played his very honorable part. But his day is done. That task is now in the very competent hands of African historians and social thinkers.

There is however a second odyssey. It is the odyssey of reconverting Western mentalities, and thereby reaching the point where Westerners take full control of their own destinies by getting the monkey off their back, the monkey of dominating others. This, I believe, is a far longer odyssey and one much more difficult of realization. One can see this in the absurd controversies that were stirred up by Edward Said's book on *Orientalism*. One can see this in the vast literature that has spewed forth in the last ten years in the US and Western Europe about "overcoming" the West's so-called guilt complex about the Third World. In that odyssey, Basil Davidson's day is not done, by any means, nor is ours.

The roots of racism are now very deep, and nowhere deeper than among Western left and liberal intellectuals, especially when they are pursuing their enlightened, progressive goals in the name both of universal science and of humanist morality. One might have thought that the history of the twentieth century—in which there were so many barbarities enacted that were far from the ideals of Enlightenment—might have had a sobering effect on the hegemonic intellectuals. But I have the feeling it has merely egged them on, to try and try again, and to be extremely defensive about anything and anyone who would call their premises into doubt. All the neo-ideologies, I fear—neo-conservatism, neo-liberalism, neo-Marxism—seem like rehashes, throwing out the frills to hold on to the essentials.

The essentials of these ideologies are not necessarily all destined for the wastebasket of history. Far from it, I believe. But they are surely due for a very thorough shaking-up. And first of all, it would be a good start to take very seriously Senghor's idea of a "rendez-vous du donner et du recevoir." African's (among others) have much to teach the West not merely about the writing of recent history but also the metaphysical presuppositions of thought and social action. Of course, the Africans must be ready to participate as equals, not subordinates. But that will come sooner than the inverse.

What can we in the West do to make more real this fundamental collective rethinking? Surely one way to start is by emulating the example of Basil Davidson—to listen, to hear, to respond. So easily said, but not easily done! To be sure, all this is not merely a matter of appropriate intellectual cogitation. The rethinking can only occur and can only be efficacious within the framework of a political struggle by the world's antisystemic movements for a socialist world order. Basil Davidson has understood this well. This is of course the intellectual link between his work on African history and his work on (and with) the contemporary liberation movements in Portuguese-speaking Africa, Eritrea, and elsewhere.

What we need to turn to therefore is the question of the degree to which the world's antisystemic movements—In Africa, in the West, in the rest of the world—have themselves broken with the metaphysical presupposition of Enlightenment thought and social action, which is at one and the same time their spiritual source and their conservative constraint. The answer is not so simple. The historic strategy of the world's antisystemic movements—change the world by acquiring state power—has been a great success and because of that an ambiguous achievement.

Let me explain. Following the only strategy that made sense, one variety or another of antisystemic movement (or of movements which came into existence to play this role, and obtained support on the basis of it) have indeed come to power in more countries than one usually thinks. And this has indeed changed the politics of a world-system as a whole and of the particular countries in which they have come to power.

But I scarcely need recount the many disillusionments following upon the many "revolutions." These disillusionments, caused by the multidinous "revisionisms," are too numerous to be ignored and far too systematic to be explained psycho-logistically as "betrayals." They are in fact structural, the consequence of the fact that all these "revolutionary" states remain, willy nilly, part and parcel of the interstate system which continues to serve as the superstructure of the capitalist world-economy. Hence the coming to power of these movements has not only undermined the world-system in all the obvious ways it was supposed to; it has only reinforced the system in less obvious (but very real) ways by participating in it and thereby making certain kinds of revolutionary struggle more, not less, difficult

This dilemma of the failures of a successful strategy is worldwide, because it is world-systemic. It is a problem precisely for the antisystemic movements. How to deal with it is the subject of a struggle within these movements. The intellectual rethinking of which we spoke is part of this struggle internal to the movements. That is, not everyone in the movements favors the break with Enlightenment thought and the West's classical version of scientific universalism. Only some do. This is the key debate of the next 25 years, one which will determine whether the demise of the capitalist world-system will in fact lead to an egalitarian socialist world order or to a new refurbished inegalitarian world-system, not capitalist but not socialist either.

Rediscovering African history is an integral part of this task. It will play its role in the internal struggle of the movements. It is therefore neither secondary nor esoteric, but a locus of the struggle for the future. Basil Davidson has helped us begin along this path. We must all go further.

12

WALTER RODNEY: THE HISTORIAN AS
SPOKESMAN FOR HISTORICAL FORCES

I have sought to ensure that the integrity of the evidence was respected at all times, for this has always to be demanded from those who practice the writing of history. Beyond that, the interpreter is himself nothing but a spokesman for historical forces.³⁵

Walter Rodney wrote three books in his life (in addition, of course, to many articles and booklets). Two of the three bore all the standard paraphernalia of scholarly history: use of archival data, footnotes, bibliography, and so on. *A History of the Upper Guinea Coast, 1545 to 1800* was his Ph.D. dissertation at SOAS and was published by Oxford University Press in 1970 (and reprinted by Monthly Review Press after his death). *A History of the Guyanese Working People, 1881-1905* (note the parallel form and traditional style of the two titles) was submitted to the publishers just months before his death, and published posthumously by Johns Hopkins University Press in 1981. The third book, *How Europe Underdeveloped Africa* (1972) was very different in style, though not in intellectual content. It is not based on archival sources, has no footnotes, and offers short annotated notes to further reading instead of a bibliography. It is openly didactic, and its intended audience is clearly university students and educated persons generally in Africa, and their friends or counterparts elsewhere. Rodney indicates his particular pleasure about the fact that his two original publishers—Bogle L'Ouverture Publications in London and Tanzania Publishing House, both "popular" publishing houses—cooperated in "publishing this volume as simply and cheaply as possible" (1972: 8).

Rereading these three books successively makes it very clear how coherent an intellectual viewpoint Rodney held, and what in a sense was his long-term intellectual agenda. He seems to me to have tackled five main themes in his corpus: capitalism as a world-system, the so-called issue of agency, the nature of the class struggle and in particular the role of non-white "middle class" elements, the structure of the working classes, and the interrelations of race and class. This is a very large agenda, and since his work was abruptly terminated at age 37 by political assassination, we will never get the further rich development of these themes of which he was obviously capable. But we have more than enough to have a clear picture of where he stood and what he was arguing. I propose to lay out Rodney's argument on each of the five themes, which seem to me to follow a certain logical order.

The starting point of his analysis, logically if not narratively, is the description of capitalism as a mode of production that concerned "the world at large which had... been transformed into a single system by the expansion of capitalist relations" (1972: 160). Within that framework, he is primarily concerned with the relationship between "underdeveloped" countries and certain "developed" ones that has been, he says, "a relationship of exploitation" (1972: 30) in which "the underdeveloped countries are dependencies of the metropolitan capitalist economies" (1972: 34). Indeed, such dependency and a "great intensification of exploitation" was the "central purpose of colonialism" (1972: 189). The interactions of the two zones had "multiplier effects" (1972: 118) that were positive for areas like Western Europe and negative for areas like Africa. The rhythms of "international capitalist forces" as reflected in economic cycles were directly and immediately felt in the underdeveloped regions, whether or not persons there were aware of this (1981: 19).

This, you may say, is old hat. Yes, it is today, to some extent, but we should recall that it was a relatively new theoretical standpoint only some 15 years ago, and Walter Rodney was one of the first to propagate it in his didactic book that was itself quite influential.

The same concept, however, is already present in the doctoral dissertation completed in 1966—in a more muted form perhaps and in a more sophisticated form, but also with considerably more empirical detail to sustain the thesis and to enable us to discern its parameters more carefully. He discusses this issue by tracing with some care the changing economic, political, and social relations on the Upper Guinea Coast from the point of first real European intrusion (that is, 1545) to 1800. As we shall see, 1800 was not an entirely fortuitous cutoff point.

In the 16th century, a number of private Portuguese traders began to reside on the coast. They were called *lançados*. They associated to their activity a small group of African slaves/ servants/wage workers called *grumetes*. The main business of the Portuguese traders was slaving; they dealt with the kings, chiefs, and nobles of various African peoples. The relationship of these rulers to the *lançados* in the 16th century was more one of host to guest than of landlord to stranger. The guests seemed to have stayed longer than expected because by the end of the century the ruling class "ceased to extend protection to the guests, and the rest of the population adopted an unfriendly attitude" (1970: 88). For one thing, the local ruling classes began to think of "gifts" as having changed from "something which was not requested and the receipt of which gave pleasant surprise, to something which was demanded, and when it was not forthcoming, this was an unpleasant surprise about which steps would be taken" (1970: 90-91). Furthermore, by the mid-17th century, European articles had begun to seem to some such "necessities" that the African intermediaries were threatening to kill the (now Spanish) captain-major if he did not allow "free trade" (1970: 129). By the mid-18th century, the exchange of presents was not only a standardized procedure but "African rulers clearly looked forward to a profit" (1970: 85).

What was happening, says Rodney, was an evolution of the basic economic process involved in the exchange. He cites Polanyi's contrast of the African model of "gainless barter" in which the exchange of equivalents was fundamental and European "market trading" for monetary profit. "In Polanyi's opinion also, it was the European system which adjusted to the African. Evidence taken from Upper Guinea helps to substantiate as well as to modify this interpretation" (1970: 192). The modification is in Rodney's insistence that the Europeans in West Africa "never relinquished" the ethos of profit accumulation, even if in daily routine they found they had to make many concessions to African practices (1970: 196).

The slave trade was the primary locus of the evolution of the basic economic process. As we know, slave trading required African intermediaries who "forcibly brought" the slaves to the Europeans. Hence there evolved a close link "between tribal wars and the slave trade." Indeed, this link accounts for "most of the inter-group hostilities" that we know about (1970: 102-103). Over time, "slave raiding became a profession" (1970: 106). In addition, customary law evolved so as to make possible the sentencing of debtors or taboo violators to sale as slaves.

This became a common fate of those accused of witchcraft as well, and, says Rodney, "the possibility for fraud in these cases were infinite" (1970: 107). Thus "the chicanery of a warped system of customary law" joined "force of arms" as the basic mode of conducting the slave trade (1970: 109).

On the other hand, slaves were never the only export, and Rodney is unhappy about the traditional temporal cleavage of a period of slave trade followed by a period of "legitimate trade." The point, he says, is that Africans were organizing themselves "to meet European demands" (1970: 157-158), which included ivory, beeswax, and camwood as well as slaves. In the case of camwood, European interest led not only to increased production but to a local processing industry. Furthermore, as early as 1691 the Royal African Company encouraged an experiment in cultivating and manufacturing indigo, which, however, was not successful.

At the same time there was a growing list of European staples being imported into the Guinea coast: metal, cloth, alcoholic beverages, weapons, and "a miscellany of baubles, bangles, and beads" (1970: 172). Rodney cautions us not to overestimate the importance of alcohol or firearms before "a very late date" (1970: 177), by which he seems to mean the second half of the 18th century. Meal and cloth for daily use were more important, but even here "local cottons ... withstood competition of European manufactures in this period" (1970: 182).

Slowly, despite the efforts of coastal intermediaries to insulate the hinterland from the Europeans in the interests of their own monopolies, the hinterland was drawn into the world-economy more directly. One result of the process was not merely the expansion of the power of the Mande peoples who controlled the slave trade but the "Mandinguization" of West African peoples (1970: 224). Major ethnic redefinitions were one mode of coping with the new economic processes. And since the Mande were not only traders but Muslims, Mandinguization involved Islamization. The renewed growth of Islam in West Africa thus is as much a function of the involvement of West Africa in the world-economy as is the growth of Christianity. Conversion to Islam presumably was a protection against being seized by other Muslims as slaves. The other Muslims in question were thereupon reluctant to recognize the legitimacy of those conversions. At this stage in the process, it could be said that at one level the Atlantic slave trade stimulated the jihad "but at a more fundamental level... [the *jihad*] was conducted with less and not greater zeal" because of the slave trade (1970: 239).

In the face of this kind of analysis, Rodney argues, "it is truly misleading to refer to African society at the end of the slave trade as 'traditional'" (1970: 259). Quite the contrary, what was described in the 19th and 20th centuries by anthropologists as African customary ways were themselves the product of a situation in which over three centuries the Upper Guinea Coast was increasingly involved in the network of "international capitalism," eventually becoming an integral part of its division of labor. This integration could be seen as becoming decisive by 1800, which is where Rodney terminates the story in his analysis of the Upper Guinea Coast.

Rodney is very sensitive to the reaction many have had to this interpretation of the history of the 1545-1800 period. Some critics have argued that it seems to imply a somewhat docile Africa being molded in some sense by an aggressive Europe. Among African historians this has been debated as the question of "agency." Were the Africans the primary "agents" of their own history, or merely reactors to other agents?

The issue of agency is not a simple one. It plagues the social sciences. As those who denigrate generalizations in the name of idiographic uniqueness never tire of saying, any structural analysis implies that an individual, a group is caught in some web not of their making and out of their control. And so it does, except that this web is in turn formed by the sum of wills that are in turn formed by the structural conditions (constraints)—a perfect circle. If one adds to this conundrum the fact that in virtually any social situation, the actors may be ranked in a hierarchy of power—some stronger, some weaker—it follows logically that the stronger "get their way" more frequently than the weaker. Else, in what sense are they stronger? This social reality is transformed into a problem of the analyst when we discuss agency. Should the analyst describe history from the top down or the bottom up? The obvious answer is the analyst should do neither, since the two are inextricably linked. The two are analytically one.

Rodney refuses to be caught in the logical traps that come from playing verbal games. He is clear on temporal sequence. On the Afro-European commercial connection on the Upper Guinea Coast, he says that

> Historically, the initiative came from Europe. It was the European commercial system which expanded to embrace the various levels of African barter economy, and to assign to them specific roles in global production. This meant the accumulation of capital from trading in Africa, and above all from the purchase of slaves and their employment in the New World. It is essential to stress that all changes on the coast occurred without prejudice to this over-all conception. Indeed, the most significant social changes on the Upper Guinea Coast demonstrated how African society became geared to serve the capitalist system [1970: 199].

Of course, it is important to note, adds Rodney, that Africa was not at that time formally colonized: "African rulers managed to maintain not simply equality but sovereignty in their personal contacts with

Europeans." However, he adds, "the commercial nexus was an entirely different matter" (1970: 253). This sovereignty was not quickly lost. Despite the "gale-force wind" of slave trading and European commercial relations, African leaders "were still making decisions before 1885...." (1972: 148).

But this temporal sequence of "initiative" is not what is analytically crucial to Rodney. This can be seen clearly in his second, didactic book. Here he spends at least half his space spelling out the ways Africa and Europe, once enlaced in a capitalist system, became a single analytic entity in which everything everywhere affected everything else. "The contention here is that [from the late 15th century on] Africa helped to develop Western Europe in the same proportion as Western Europe helped to underdevelop Africa" (1972: 85). Rodney was always a careful formulator of his own position. He was aware of the high level of generality of such a statement. He took pains to make it more precise:

> It would be extremely simple-minded to say that colonialism in Africa or anywhere else caused Europe to develop its science and technology. The tendency towards technological innovation and renovation was inherent in capitalism itself, because of the drive for profits. However, it would be entirely accurate to say that the colonisation of Africa and other parts of the world formed an indispensable link in a chain of events which made possible the technological transformation of the base of European capitalism. Without that link, European capitalism would not have been producing goods and services at the level attained in 1960. In other words, our very yardsticks for measuring developed and underdeveloped nations would have been different [1972: 190].

Within this capitalist system, persons in the periphery pursued their interests as well as they could, and Rodney was always concerned "to identify the local changes that modified the picture of underdevelopment as sheer stagnation" (1981: 217). Nonetheless, the most salient reality was that the capitalist world-economy was structured around a core-periphery antinomy, and this meant that the zone that was "developed" not only was the locus of installation of the new technology but of the growth of employment opportunities. "The mining that went on in Africa left holes in the ground, and the pattern of agricultural production left African soils impoverished; but, in Europe, agricultural and mineral imports built a massive industrial complex" (1972: 197). For Africa, the impact of colonial rule was negative not only economically but politically. And one of its worst effects, says Rodney, was the spread of capitalist individualism:

> The idea of individualism was more destructive in colonial Africa than it was in metropolitan capitalist society. In the latter, it could be said that the rise of the bourgeois class indirectly benefitted the working classes, through promoting technology and raising the standard of living. But, in Africa, colonialism did not bring those benefits—it merely intensified the rate of exploitation of African labor and continued to export the surplus. In Europe, individualism led to entrepreneurship and adventurism of the type which spearheaded Europe's conquest of the rest of the world. In Africa, both the formal school system and the informal value system of colonialism destroyed social solidarity and promoted the worst form of alienated individualism without social responsibility. That delayed the political process through which the society tried to regain its independence [1972: 280].

It is in the light of this analysis of the cultural process that Rodney deals with the role of the non-white "middle classes." From the very outset, class differences in the periphery were crucial, argues Rodney: "in its contacts with Europeans, the African society of the Upper Guinea Coast did not present itself as an undifferentiated entity. The patterns of trade often transcended tribal divisions, but never the distinction between *fidalgo* [noble] and plebeian" (1970: 38). First of all, from the outset, the European traders "always dealt with the kings, chiefs, and nobles" and therefore it was no accident that the groups who "were the least developed as far as their state structure was concerned" were also the groups "who were the slowest to forge relations with the Europeans" (1970: 82-83). And the long-term consequences of this were to accentuate still further class polarization within African groups:

> It is a striking fact that the great agents of the Atlantic slave trade, the Mande and the Fulas, were the very elements who subsequently continued to handle the internal slave trade, and whose society came to include significant numbers of disprivileged individuals laboring under coercion....

> One of the most direct connections between the Atlantic slave trade and the nineteenth-century pattern of social stratification lay in the fact that some Africans were captured with a view to being sold to European slavers, but they remained for greater or lesser periods (or sometimes forever) in the service of their African captors. To begin with, there was usually a time lag between capture and the moment when a buyer presented himself. Then there were always individuals whom Europeans rejected for one reason or another; while African merchants also decided against carrying through the sale under certain circumstances [1970: 264].

By and large, the nobility was inviolate. They were not normally seized by the slave raiders and, if captured, could be ransomed. This served not only the interests of the nobles but also of the Europeans, by allowing them to trade simultaneously with various neighboring peoples, each one selling its neighbors and the nobles being safe. Rodney calls this "the harmonization of the cupidity of all who stood to gain" (1970: 116) and argues that the line of demarcation between the agents and victims of slaving coincided consequently with "the distinction between the privileged and unprivileged in the society as a whole." He then concludes that "This is of course the widespread pattern of modern neo-colonialism; and by the same token the period of slave trading in West Africa should be regarded as proto-colonial" (1970: 117-118). In addition to the nobility who became the political intermediaries of the Europeans, there arose a group of mulatto traders. These mixed-blood descendants of Portuguese male traders became the core of a new African commercial stratum. From their fathers they inherited wealth and, even more importantly, commercial expertise.

> Afro-Europeans were aware that they straddled two worlds, and that there was advantage to be gained by identifying themselves with one or the other, as circumstances dictated. Of James Cleveland, Matthews had this to say, 'To sum up his character in a few words: with a White Man he is a White Man, with a Black Man a Black Man'.
>
> This then was the efficient comprador class of the Upper Guinea Coast in a proto-colonial situation. They squeezed Africans to make as much personal profit as possible, but essentially they served the wider interests of European commercial capitalism [1970: 221-222].

The nature of the African material of the pre-1800 period is such that it permitted Rodney to analyze in some detail this *comprador* class, but he was able to say much less about the un-privileged majority. He more than compensated for this imbalance when he came to treat Guyana in the period 1881-1905. Indeed, the very title tells us that he intends to focus on what he calls the "working people." Nor is it some slip that led him to use the uncommon locution. His entire treatment of the Guyanese working people is one that calls into question the traditional lines between urban proletarian and rural peasant. By looking closely at the Guyanese working people—the urban and rural ones simultaneously—in the period immediately following slave emancipation, he discovered social patterns that were different from conventional accounts (of Guyana, first of all, and then of peripheral zones generally).

Slavery did not come to an end in the Caribbean, Rodney reminds us, because the slave masses rose up to defeat and crush their masters. It ended "mainly because of having exhausted itself politically and economically in terms of the system of international exchange." The planters/estate owners remained the most powerful and influential economic actors in Guyana throughout the 19th century. The end of slavery merely gave them a problem of how to realize profits "while making the minimum of concessions to the newly emancipated population" (1981: 31).

How could they do this? Not at all by the "untrammeled operation of free wage labor" to which the planters were "bitterly opposed" (1981: 32). But why should capitalists—and Rodney never doubts for an instant that 19th-century Guyanese planters were capitalists—be bitterly opposed to the untrammeled operation of free wage labor? Obviously because it would have reduced their ability to accumulate capital. Rodney's whole book is an attempt to explicate why this is so.

The heart of the analysis, Rodney makes very clear in the conclusion, is that "the Guyanese working class constituted itself through its own activities" (1981: 220). This may seem a curious way to put it, or at least one to which we are not used. It is made even more curious by this observation:

> Planters seemed not to recognize that productivity and the cost of living were crucial variables which should have altered the rate of wages; and it was left to the workers to take up a stance that was much closer to modern concepts of industrial relations in the capitalist world itself [1981: 197].

The world seems upside down in this analysis. The working people constitute themselves as a proletariat, and are not forced to this state by the capitalists? And these same workers express, or at least call on, the functional values of the system more than the capitalist? Yes, Rodney does mean to say this.

His arguments draw on a close analysis of what happened on the sugar plantations after slavery. The rural wage earners there are often imprecisely designated as "peasants" (1981: 60). In fact, ex-slaves did not become "peasants" after Emancipation, but rather "plantation workers" (1981: 218), and this of three main varieties: "bound" or indentured laborers, free estate residents, and village laborers. This trifold division was a hierarchy or continuum from low to high in terms of skills, freedom, bargaining power, and wage levels. Naturally, the plantation owners therefore preferred indentured labor. The workers themselves wanted to be or to become village laborers, who were the closest of the three to being full proletarians; hence, it can be said that the workers sought to *advance themselves* to the status of proletarians.

What were the tactics of the capitalist plantation owners? They put pressure on the government to facilitate the import of indentured labor (from the East Indies). They constantly complained they were too "expensive" (although they were in fact the least expensive labor on the market). These complaints were in part a way of getting the state to bear part of the wage bill and in part a tactic in the effort to guarantee "planter *control* over the entire labor process" (1981: 39).

Village labor organized itself in independent task gangs that moved from estate to estate and "negotiated with management to have some control over wages, conditions, and duration of work" (1981: 43). Management had two main weapons. One was indentureship that "altered the market conditions for free labor in favor of the planters" (1981: 44). The second was the variable state of the world sugar market. The planters, of course, "held the upper hand during the slack periods in the [annual] crop cycle" (1981: 47). But even more tellingly, they held the upper hand every time there were international price falls that provided "the most powerful sanction on the side of capital in keeping village labor under a tight rein" (1981: 49).

Rodney reproduces for us a notice put up on an estate in September, 1896:

> Owing to the exceedingly LOW price of SUGAR, the lowest that has ever been known, it is ABSOLUTELY IMPOSSIBLE for us to pay the Old Rate of Wages and Carry the Estate on; I am aware that even the Old Rates were a reduced rate, but under the circumstances there is nothing for it but to still further reduce all round. It is a hard thing to ask, but if the Laborers and Mechanics will cheerfully accept the Reduction there is just a hope for the Estate and nothing more. If they refuse we must close up, and that almost at once. Should Prices rise to a paying level I need hardly say that I will give back what has been cutoff [1981: 50].

We are, of course, familiar these days with this tactic. Automobile manufacturers, steel corporations, and airlines use it to extract wage reductions from powerful unions in the United States.

What weapons were at the disposition of the Guyanese working people? The same one as elsewhere: they could withhold their labor. Since this could be countered in the marketplace by the import of indentured labor, they could only do this to the extent that their labor was more skilled and therefore rarer. In these cases, they might be effective. The freer labor therefore made factory labor as opposed to field labor their preserve, and within field labor, they were "sparsely represented" in the lowest-paid, least-skilled jobs (weeding, for example) and played a "strategically decisive role" in the better-paid, most-skilled jobs (such as cane-cutting or punt-loading) (1981: 44). When a work stoppage was threatened, the plantation owners sought to substitute an indentured gang for the independent task gang, but they were constrained by two considerations: the difference in specializations (that is, in skills) and the fact that indentured gangs "constituted a burden during the out-of-crop season" (1981: 48).

The outcome of this constant struggle was the widespread institutionalization of "part-time labor" that "both class protagonists used... as a weapon" (1981: 47). That is, part-time labor was in effect a compromise position. This meant for the laborers' household a wide mix of occupations:

> Taking the household as a unit, it is all the more clear that village labor covered an extremely wide spectrum, from domestic service through to the panning of gold in stream beds. Examples of the combination and overlap of farmer and balata bleeder or sugar worker and diamond seeker were extremely common. They support the contention of this analysis that former slaves did not simply become peasants after Emancipation. They became instead potential members of a free labor force and were amenable to numerous forms of labor. Pressures generated by international depression caused Indian workers to use rice farming to enhance monetary earnings, while Africans resorted to the bush for their survival and created a new economic sector [1981: 102].

Eventually, the sugar estates would collapse because of loss to international competition, and the locus of economic development in Guyana moved to the hinterland and to other products. Some of the rural wage earners now became real peasants but in a system that proceeded rapidly "toward stratification based on dispossession of the many and accumulation of the few" (1981: 106). A few moved to towns and became artisans, "a little less poor" (1981: 112). Most eventually became urban workers.

This process of partially self-willed proletarianization accentuated the "racial" segregation of the working class. The Black Creole workers moved off the estates, leaving behind the Indian indentured workers who later became free estate residents.

> The availability or nonavailability of land for peasant farming was another major issue that proved racially divisive. The white-dominated plantation society was unrelenting in its vindictiveness against Creole small farmers. Without displaying any greater love for time-expired Indian peasants, the system nevertheless found it advisable to accommodate some Indian demands for land. This was done at the expense of Creole Africans—sometimes quite literally by replacing one group by the other. Parate execution sales facilitated the concentration of rural property in fewer hands. Simultaneously, it sparked off a transfer from Creole Africans as a group into the hands of Indians, Portuguese, and Chinese....

> When lands were sold for nonpayment of rates and taxes, the colonial government simply sold to those who could afford it out of trading profits or from accumulated savings. Indentured and unindentured immigrants had to practice considerable self-denial in order to save. From an Indian perspective, all land purchases were legitimate and helped in a small way to meet a great need. Politically, the planter class succeeded in interposing another set of landowners between itself and its traditional villagized African antagonists of the post-Emancipation era [1981: 182].

In this way the capitalists sought to use African and Indian attempts to improve their conditions against each other and thereby create a racial division that Rodney argues is not endemic and "has been overstated" (1981: 188). In any case, one cannot understand the forms it has taken except in the context of the attempts by the capitalists to control labor and the working people to pursue their class interests.

Thus Rodney ends where he began, with a class analysis, but one centrally located within the operations of a singular capitalist world-economy, in which it is the capitalists, not the working people, who are resisting the process of full proletarianization because of the fact that it threatens to diminish, not increase, their possibilities of capital accumulation. Such an intellectual analysis has clear political implications for the organization of the working people. Rodney tried to live out these implications, and was assassinated because of them.

References

Walter Rodney, *A History of the Upper Guinea Coast, 1545 to 1800*. Oxford: Clarendon Press, 970.

_____. *How Europe Underdeveloped Africa*. London and Dar es Salaam: Bogle-L'Ouverture Publications and Tanzania Publishing House, 1972.

_____. *A History of the Guyanese Working People, 1881-1905*. Baltimore: Johns Hopkins University Press, 1981.

13

OLIVER C. COX AS WORLD-SYSTEMS ANALYST

Oliver Cox, writing ten years before the persons usually identified as the originators of a world-systems perspective, in fact argued a set of five propositions about historical capitalism which agrees in all essential points with the world-systems perspective: (1) capitalism is not merely a system; it is a *world*-system; (2) capitalism operates as a capitalist world-economy, based on the endless accumulation of capital; (3) there is an axial division of labor in the capitalist world-economy, based on the core-periphery antinomy; (4) there inevitably occurred a steady shift in the location of the central states in the system; (5) capitalism was not invented multiple times, but only once.

In 1987, Paul Sweezy wrote:

> Particularly noteworthy is the fact that after Cox's death a whole new branch of historical sociology, generally known as world systems theory, opened up and rapidly grew in the Americas, under the leadership of such eminent scholars as Immanuel Wallerstein, Andre Gunder Frank, and Samir Amin. Both chronologically and logically, Oliver Cox deserves to be considered not only as a forerunner but a founding father of this relatively new and welcome departure in American sociology (Sweezy 1987, p. x).

I agree. Oliver Cox expounded in the 1950s and 1960s virtually all the basic ideas of world-systems analysis. He is a founding father, albeit one who is hardly recognized as such and is widely neglected, even today. Let us hope that this essay does something to repair this grievous oversight.

If Oliver Cox has a reputation, it is largely for his first major work, *Caste, Class, and Race*. Few scholars are even aware that he subsequently wrote a trilogy on capitalism. I think, however, that the publication sequence is important in understanding Cox's contribution. Cox, a Trinidadian who migrated to the United States, sought to understand the nature of racism, particularly the more virulent form he discovered here. In seeking an explanation, he decided that the principal analyses current at the time he was writing were pernicious. He was particularly unhappy for various reasons with the use of "caste" as an explanatory variable, primarily because it failed to distinguish a mode of stratification (caste) which had long existed in some pre-modern historical systems (and, of course, particularly in the Indian world) and the racism he confronted in the modern world-system. He decided that the crucial difference between caste and race as mechanisms of stratification derived from the fact that racism was an invention of the modern world, and the modern world was a capitalist world:

> Racial antagonism is part and parcel of [the] class struggle, because it developed within the capitalist system as one of its fundamental traits. It may be demonstrated that racial antagonism, as we know it today, never existed in the world before about 1492; moreover, racial feeling developed concomitantly with the development of our modern social system (Cox 1959a, p. xxx).

Cox thus came to believe that one must analyze capitalism as a *system*, seeing it as the container within which racism was created and nourished. This, of course, had implications for the political struggle to end racism. Cox clearly believed that racism would persist as long as capitalism persisted, and that it would only end (or at least could only end) when capitalism no longer survived. Marxist or not Marxist (I leave to others this theological dispute), his was a radical point of view, and especially radical coming from a Black intellectual—and even more threatening because it came from a Black intellectual who was clearly a careful, well-read scholar, one whose scientific credentials were not that easy to challenge. It is no wonder that conservative forces sought to muffle his voice. If one adds to the equation his own quiet conventional cultural style (his was not the stentorian bombast of a tribune), we can understand why even Black radicals of the 1970s tended to ignore him. Still, it is a pity and a loss.

Cox was determined to bring together two quite separate literatures, the sociology of race (race relations, racism) and the economic history of the modern world. Neither, he felt, could be adequately explored without the other. Cox was quite explicit that he was in no way suggesting the merits of an inverse racism:

> It should be made clear that we do not mean to say that the white race is the only one capable of race prejudice. It is probable that without capitalism, a cultural chance occurrence among whites, the world might never have experienced race prejudice (Cox 1959a, p. 345).

Note the phrase "capitalism, a cultural chance occurrence among whites." We shall return to it. But note also the clear rejection of the idea that there is some inherent cultural tendency towards racism among Whites/Europeans. This is the heart of his ferocious rejection of Black cultural nationalism, which led to much misunderstanding, and which was firmly expressed in his final work, *Race Relations: Elements and Social Dynamics*.

And why is there racial prejudice in a capitalist social system? Cox is again very explicit when he discusses the limitations of Robert Park's analysis of race prejudice in the United States:

> [I]n the United States the race problem developed out of the need of the planter class, the ruling class, to keep the freed Negro exploitable. To do this, the ruling class had to do what every ruling must do; that is, develop mass support for its policy. Race prejudice was and is the convenient vehicle....
>
> Race prejudice in the United States is the socio-attitudinal matrix supporting a calculated and determined effort of a white ruling class to keep some people or peoples of color and their resources exploitable. In a quite literal sense the white ruling class is the Negro's burden; the saying that the white man will do anything for the Negro except get off his back puts the same idea graphically (Cox 1959a, p. 475).

But, adds Cox, speaking of Gobineau, it is not merely an internal U.S. problem. Quite the opposite! The international dimension is central to racism:

> Class conflict and capitalism are inseparable, modern race relations developed out of the imperialistic practices of capitalism, while offensive and defensive nationalism provides the *esprit de corps* necessary for solidarity in exploitative group action under capitalism (Cox 1959a, p. 483).

Much as Cox rejects the idea that racism is culturally inherent in the West, and much as he thinks that capitalism was culturally accidental in the West, he emphatically believes that capitalism originated in the West: "Capitalism developed in Europe exclusively; in the East it is a cultural adoption" (Cox 1959a, p. 485).

I have deliberately developed my argument thus far by using only quotations from Cox's first book, the one on race published in 1948. Obviously, his concern with and analysis of capitalism is already prefigured there, but of course not in the detail that the subsequent trilogy (1959-1964) was to elaborate. The degree to which Cox's analysis parallels that of later world-systems analysts is quite remarkable. I shall indicate this by developing a series of propositions found in Cox which are identified with world-systems analysis.

1. Capitalism is not merely a system; it is a *world*-system.

> Economically, capitalism tends to form a system or network of national and territorial units bound together by commercial and exploitative relationships in such a way that a capital is t nation is inconceivable outside this capitalist-system (l959b, p. 15).

> This tendency, of capitalism to form a highly integrated, universal structure is perhaps its most remarkable trait (1962, p. xiii).

> If it is recognized that the internal economy of the United States is inseparably tied into a world system [this is one of the few times Cox actually uses the term 'world system'], then not only its progressive dependence on military expenditures but also its relationship to the extremely low standard of living in the backward countries of the system would readily become apparent (1962, pp. xvi-xvii).

2. Capitalism operates as a capitalist world-economy, based on the endless accumulation of capital.

> But what is distinctive of capitalism is that, under it, the great businessman does not work simply to make a good living; he must constantly augment his wealth through profits, or perish (1964, p. 35).

> It is necessary to bear in mind that an inherent characteristic of the capitalist system is its boundless scope. To conceive of it as being circumscribed in some national economy is to misapprehend all its typical traits. Capitalist economies must either expand abroad or stagnate. They cannot be shut-in like feudalism. Most of the major errors of classical and Marxian economics are rooted in an implied or expressed assumption that capitalism can be conceived of as a closed system (1962, p. xiv).

Indeed, his principal critique of Marx was of the Marx who had not sufficiently liberated himself from the premises of classical economics, the Marx who did not sufficiently emphasize capitalism as a world-system:

> [Marx] begins his analysis of the nature of capitalism almost where he might have ended it; and as is commonly the case in classical economics, he relegates as subsidiary the very things which should have been the center of his study.... His 'primitive accumulation' is none other than fundamentally capitalist accumulation; and to assume that feudal society dissolved before capitalist society began is to over-emphasize the fragility of feudalism and to discount its vises to the development of capitalism....
>
> According to Marx, the criterion of capitalist development in England was industrial development....
>
> If Marx had comprehended the entire capitalist system with its foreign impulsions and sources of wealth available to the leading capitalist nations, he might not have been so satisfied with this industrial explanation of the growth of capital (1964, pp. 213-215).

In this skepticism about industrial production being the defining element in capitalism—he calls industrialization "an accelerator of capitalist tendencies" (1959b, p. 456)—Cox joins Schumpeter, Braudel, and later world-systems analysts:

> One popular classification which could lead to vast misunderstandings about the progress of modern urbanism is that of representing the industrial revolution as a historical break (1959b, p. 28).
>
> The [industrial] "revolution" was in fact largely a quantitative change, the high value put upon improvements goes back to the early cities (1959b, p. 406).
>
> [W]e shall attempt to demonstrate that all capitalism is essentially commercial. Industry has an important but peculiar place in capitalist society (1959b, p. 75).

Cox's resistance to seeing industry as the key element derives from the same source as would that of Braudel—the disbelief that capitalists specialize:

> For itself, the leader capitalist nation tends to abhor specialization; it strains toward diversification of production (1964, p. 110).
>
> England began to provide the basic needs of food, clothing, and housing to distant peoples; thus vastly expanding and strengthening interdependence of communities in the capitalist system. Furthermore, since the production of backward peoples became more and more specialized, their entire social organization and way of life became increasingly exposed to the will of the diversified manufacturing nations (1959b, p. 441).

And Cox emphasizes, precisely as do Braudel and later world-systems analysts, the crucial role of monopoly in capitalist profit:

> Like all leading capitalist communities the center of Hanseatic interests always resided in its monopolistic commercial position (1959b, p. 194).

It was the world-system-ness of capitalism that enhanced the monopolies:

> Distant trade, moreover, brought the market to relatively non-competitive areas; hence ignorance of the market made monopoly prices possible (1959b, p. 358).

To be dynamic, capitalists must be dynamic and worldwide in scope:

> We shall be continually brought to emphasize the point... that foreign commerce is indispensable to a capitalist nation. The capitalist nation

must trade or perish. This fact is exemplified in Venetian experience, as it is in vital international problems of our own day (1959b, p. 71).

By definition, leadership in the capitalist system means domination of the foreign commerce of the world. This domination tends to reduce the leader's dependence upon economic changes in any one country, but not upon broad movements in the system (1964, p. 129).

And capital flows essentially to, rather than from, leading capitalist zones. To be sure, "the size and form of foreign investment tend to correlate directly with national leadership... [but] the leader nation tends also to be the largest importer of capital" (1964, p. 164). The reason is very simple; capital is safer there: "foreigners sought, as a privilege, to invest in these gilt-edged securities" (1959b, p. 81). And, adds Cox, not only capital but also skilled labor flows to the core:

Like all future leading capitalist nations, Venice continually attracted foreign workers. Because of her extensive control of markets, her demand for labor was greater. The coming of the skilled workers from Lucca is not unlike the later immigration of the Huguenots to the capitalist towns of northern Europe. To put it in modern terms, Venice, in her day, was 'God's own country' (1959b, p. 77).

3. There is an axial division of labor in the capitalist world-economy, based on the core-periphery antinomy. (Although Cox has a very clear notion of this division of labor, he does not use the core-periphery language, of which he seems to be unaware.)

An implied proposition of this work... is that the capitalist system rests upon a broad base of backward countries.... This is so because the existence of capitalism in the leader countries is unthinkable in complete isolation from their peculiar, sometimes indirect affiliations with these countries (1962, p. 121).

One obvious, though vital conclusion to be drawn from this relationship is that capitalism does not and cannot mean the same thing to all nations and territories included in the system. At one extreme it may mean for whole peoples a higher standard of living, greater freedom, and a more complete existence than mankind has even before enjoyed; at the other it may mean, for great masses of people, grinding poverty, racial humiliation, and the lash (1964, p. xi).

> The interrelated societies of the system in their various stages of development have unequal power and unequal opportunities in the market. Thus leadership of the system implies particularly dominance in its most coveted foreign markets (1962, p. xiv).

Indeed, not only do capitalist centers require this relation to "backward countries," but it turns out that it is the single most important element in their strength.

> Indeed, it seems that capitalism itself depends pivotally neither upon the market situation among advanced capitalist nations, nor upon domestic transactions, but rather upon the economic and political relations developing between the major capitalist nations and the backward peoples. Here lies the heart of the imbalance and elasticity of capitalist market situations. There is no substitute for it. When Venice lost its eastern trade and the Hansa its *kontors*, they both lost their traditional status as capitalist powers. Both needed the products which each acquired abroad, not particularly for domestic consumption but to support their profitable circle of external commerce (1964, p. 8).

Nor was this true only of the early days of the capitalist world-system. It was equally true in Cox's day.

> The United States as a consequence of its leadership, sits at the top of an international structure which rests upon a broad base of backward economies (1962, p. xvii).

Seen from the perspective of the poorer nations, the capitalist world-economy was like a spider's web:

> Once the economy of non-capitalist peoples has been brought into the markets of the system, it tends rapidly to lose its capacity to subsist outside the system (1964, p. 103).

The historically continuing reality of this unequal relation between core and periphery leads to an open rejection of the Hobson-Lenin argument that imperialism is a product of late capitalism. Quite the contrary:

> Imperialism… seems to be an abiding attribute of capitalism. It is not, as sometimes thought, a late nineteenth century development; rather,

> it has gone hand in hand with the rise of the capitalist system as a necessary component (1964, p. 136).

> Imperialism... is by means a nugatory excrescence of capitalism; it has, on the contrary, provided its very base, its broad structural underpinning. Accordingly, then, this realization has led all leading capitalist nations properly to associate their imperialist position with their destiny. Since leader nations always seek to secure the lion's share in all new ventures abroad, there can be no room for contentment with existing possessions (1964, p. 138).

> There is... a capitalist strain toward colonization, the essentials of which should be distinguished from colonization among the ancients (1959b, p. 74).

The centrality of colonization/imperialism to capitalism leads Cox to a forthright position on slavery and the slave trade:

> [T]he Venetian slave trade was the first capitalistically organized commerce in human beings. Slavery, to be sure, existed from time immemorial, but early in her career Venice brought the traffic within the system of her commodity exchanges and defended it against sporadic mora attacks principally from the Church at Rome (1959b, p. 70).

> The slave trade was an extreme situation in the capitalist exploitation of all labor; its principles fitted nicely into the same pattern of interests which conceived of the common people at home as "vicious," and which later developed racial hate and prejudice against all exploitable peoples of color (1959b, p. 385).

It follows, from Cox's belief that capitalism is built around transnational economic relations, and that imperialism/colonialism is a fundamental structural element in the system, that Cox believes that interstate political relations are central to the analysis of how capitalism functions.

> Economically, capitalism tends to form a network of national and territorial units bound together by commercial and exploitative relationships in such a way that a capitalist nation is inconceivable outside this capitalist system (1959b, p. 15).

> The active element in the maintenance and ordering of the capitalist system is principally the organization of consuls and ambassadors.... Capitalist commerce indicates the need for ambassadors and consuls as permanent institutions; and their function becomes distinct from that of, say, the representatives of feudal rulers (1959b, p. 102),

Nationalism is viewed as a political stance within the interstate system:

> Nationalism... presupposes a world system of unequal national units cooperating antagonistically, as well as of localized citizens whose interests are inextricably bound up with the fate of their country. In other words, nationalism is generated by the peculiar international competition and rivalry existing within the capitalist system (1964, p. 27).

And this nationalism was indeed national, appealing to all classes and not restricted to the capitalist strata:

> The working class in a leading nation... has sufficient reason to walk arm in arm with its oligarchy against the world. On imperialist questions, we should ordinarily expect this class to be nationalistic, because a threat to the imperial position of the nation tends to become a threat to its own welfare. The class struggle thus goes on at home... for a larger share of the national income. But it is a struggle that tends to stop at the water's edge where antagonisms with rival imperialisms and exploited backward peoples begin (1964, p. 194).

This conception of nationalism reflecting the centrality of interstate competition between states within the capitalist system led Cox, along with other world-systems analysts, to a clear perception of the role of mercantilism historically within the system. Mercantilism is the tactic, neither of the leading state nor of the least powerful ones, but precisely of those of the second rank:

> Mercantilism does not come into existence in backward capitalist communities, because in these communities the element of dynamic capitalist aspiration and the probability of visualizing themselves as leading capitalist nations are lacking (1959b, p. 324).

> The period of mercantilism begins... somewhere near to the time when capitalists of a country realize that it is possible to convert their territory into an independent national unit and pilot it to leadership in the capitalist system by instituting the societal practices already largely tried with success in existing capitalist communities (1959b, p. 393).

> It should be recognized at the outset that the mercantilists were interested primarily in the status of their nation relatively to all other countries and peoples of the world.... The mercantilists realized clearly

and stated frankly that there is a system in international commerce and that the nation must either lead or be led (1959b, pp. 330-331).

The mercantilists were clearly correct, in the judgment of Cox, for they had a sound understanding of the functioning of the capitalist world-economy:

> The mercantilists recognized two significant relationships in capitalist economy: the dependence of domestic commerce upon foreign trade, and the pivotal role of manufacturers in foreign trade. They would never have accepted the non-societal critique of Smith that: "the inland or home trade [was] the most important of all trade" even if it could be shown by simple addition that the total number of domestic transactions amounted to a much larger commercial turnover than that of imports and exports. The mercantilist saw domestic commerce as a partial but important support of foreign commerce.... The general attitude seems to have been that, in the actual state of international rivalry, foreign trade and home production were indispensably associated, with the foreign-trade element providing the dynamic spark (1959b, pp. 365-366).

Thus mercantilism was the tactic of the runner-up (or should we call it the catcher-up?).

4. There occurred inevitably a steady shift in the location of the central state in the system.

> The decline of a leading capitalist society tends to follow a certain recognizable cycle which appears to be characteristic of the phenomenon. Both Venice and the Hanseatic League... were superseded by Holland, and the latter in turn by England (1959b, p. 129).

And the explanation of this constant shift lies not so much in the lessening of the merits of the leader, as in the increase of the merits of the rivals.

> After about 1650, however, the tide began to ebb. The decline of Holland was caused not by a shifting of great trade routes or even by exhaustion of national resources, but by sheer force of rivalry in rising powers.... The falling back of the United Provinces was gradual; indeed, in some respects, she moved forward only more slowly than her great rivals (1959b, p. 244).

Finally, the erstwhile leading country declines, but not all that abruptly. For example, speaking of the United Provinces, Cox notes:

> Her colonial possessions were so extensive and rich that, even with the loss of leadership, the country rested upon a great cushion of prosperity; grass did not grow in the streets as in Antwerp. Moreover, Holland continued to be integrated in the rapidly expanding capitalist system. Now that her own drive abroad was checked, her accumulated wealth sought employment in the capital markets of Europe (1959b, p. 244).

And this tactic allowed for a slow, dignified, but very real lapse into the sunset. Speaking of Venice, Cox notes:

> She exhibited another typical characteristic of declining capitalist society: the tendency to export capital to the new leader for more efficient uses. She had already ceased not only to be an attraction for foreign funds but also for investment of her own accumulated resources. The former industrious merchants now largely became rentiers, investing in foreign securities and land, and living in luxury. The skilled workman was no longer the prize he used to be; for he had fallen behind his congeners of other nations in the use of new techniques. Therefore, while funds moved easily to Holland, workmen with traditional skills were less mobile and suffered particular hardships. Even so, however, there was considerable emigration, and the city was ultimately left to recline in faded glory, no doubt the greatest relic of early capitalist culture (1959b, p. 131).

I think the reader will see clearly by now how consonant Cox's mode of analysis of capitalism is with what has come to be called world-systems analysis. Furthermore, it should be noted that this is not merely true of the major lines of the analysis of the system as a system, but on the relationship of the system to the whole of world history.

5. Capitalism was not invented multiple times, but only once.

> The [capitalist] system ... had only one origin. Previously non-capitalist communities became capitalist as their internal organizations, especially their economic structures, became critically meshed with the imperious functions of the system (1964, p. xi).

The crucial question, then, is: When and where do we locate the origins of capitalism? This is a matter of some debate among world-systems analysts. And Cox himself is not always clear on the subject. The most definitive statement is in favor of the thirteenth century "as the period when capitalism became definitely established in the world [because] by this date the culture had become irreversible" (1959b, p. 126; see also 1964, p. 287). It is important to note that he decides on this date in terms of what he calls culture, that is, on the primacy of the endless accumulation of capital as the decisive element in the system.

It is at this point that we should remember his statement: "capitalism, a chance occurrence among whites." He does not elaborate on what made it a "chance occurrence," but he seems clearly to suggest that there was nothing in the prior culture of Venetians or West Europeans or anyone in particular that accounts for the onset of the system, that the "culture" of the system, however crucial, was a consequence and not a cause. Regrettably, nowhere in Cox's analysis do we have a discussion of exactly why this "chance" occurrence occurred when and where it did.

One may wonder, after this essay, why Cox's contributions have not been widely discussed. I have pondered this. It is true that he published the key work, *Foundations of Capitalism*, in 1959, just a little too early to be caught up in the reading tide of 1968. But there is another reason. Cox, I have already said, wished to bring together two literatures, that of race and that of economic history. For the latter, this meant principally the classical economists and Marx, the German historical school, and conventional English economic history. As far as one can tell, he did not read in the two literatures that most influenced world-systems analysis. On the one hand, although he had read Pirenne, mostly in translation, he did not seem to have read the *Annales* school—Febvre, Bloch, and especially Braudel. On the other hand, he does not seem to have followed the post-1945 literature of the economic development of backward/underdeveloped/peripheral areas, and in particular Prebisch (and his associates at ECLA, the Economic Commission for Latin America) plus the *dependistas*. Thus the paths of Cox and the authors who were later to be identified with world-systems analysis did not pass each other. There was much mutual ignorance, and combined with the lapse of a decade, Cox and the other authors did not fructify one another. But it is not too late for them to do so now.

References

Oliver C. Cox. *Caste, Class, and Race: A Study in Social Dynamics*. New York: Monthly Review Press, 1959a (1948).

_____. *The Foundations of Capitalism*. London: Peter Owen, 1959b.

_____. *Capitalism and American Leadership*. New York: Philosophical Library, 1962.

_____. *Capitalism as a System*. New York: Monthly Review Press, 1964.

_____. *Race Relations: Elements and Social Dynamics*. Detroit: Wayne State University Press, 1976.

P. M. Sweezy. Foreword to H. M. Hunter and S. Y. Abraham (eds.), *Race, Class, and the World System: The Sociology of Oliver C. Cox* (pp. ix-xi). New York: Monthly Review Press, 1987.

14

READING FANON IN THE 21ˢᵀ CENTURY

"I belong irreducibly to my time," wrote Frantz Fanon in his first book, *Black Skin, White Masks*. That time was, of course, the era of anti-colonial struggles. Born in the then French colony of Martinique in 1925, where he was a student of Aimé Césaire, Fanon fought with the Allied forces in the Second World War and then trained in Lyon as a physician and psychiatrist. His remarkable *Black Skin, White Masks* was published in 1952 and had a significant impact in intellectual circles in France at the time. It was a passionate *cri de cœur*—"the experience of a black man thrown into a white world."[36] In 1953 Fanon was appointed to the Blida Psychiatric Hospital in Algeria, just a year before the outbreak of the War of Independence. He rapidly became outraged by the stories of torture that his Algerian patients recounted to him. Already a sympathizer with their cause, he resigned his post and went to Tunisia to work full time for the Gouvernement Provisoire de la République Algérienne (GPRA). He wrote extensively for *El Moudjahid*, the official journal of the revolution.

In 1960, the GPRA sent him as its ambassador to Ghana, at that time the *de facto* center of the movement for African unity. The GPRA wanted him to reinforce links not only with Ghana, but with the various nationalist movements in Africa still struggling for their independence, and whose leaders regularly passed through Accra. It was there that I first met Fanon in 1960 and where we had long discussions about the world political situation. He was both very encouraged by the global sweep of the national liberation movements, and disturbed by the signs he saw already in the limitations of the leadership of many of these movements—discomforts he would discuss at length in his last book. Soon thereafter, he fell ill of leukemia. He went first to the Soviet Union and then to the United States for treatments, which were fruitless. I was able to visit him in hospital in Washington, where we discussed the nascent Black Power movement in the United States with which he was fascinated. He exploded with anger about us policies in the world. He said "Americans are not engaged in dialogue; they still speak monologues." In the last year of his life, he devoted himself principally and furiously to writing the book published posthumously as *The Wretched of the Earth*.[37] Fanon lived to read the famous preface by Jean-Paul Sartre, which he thought superb. The title of the book, *Les damnés de la terre*, was, of course, drawn from the opening lines of the Internationale, the song of the world workers' movement. He died, much too young, in 1961.

It was this work, not *Black Skin, White Masks*, which brought Fanon his world reputation, including of course in the United States. The book became something like a bible for all those involved in the many and diverse movements that culminated in the world revolution of 1968. After the initial flames of 1968 died out, *Wretched of the Earth* receded into a quieter corner. In the late 1980s, the various identity and post-colonial movements discovered his first book, upon which they lavished attention, much of it missing Fanon's point. As he wrote in the Introduction to *Black Skin, White Masks*, Fanon thought that to overcome the alienation of the black man would require more than what Freudian psychoanalysis had to offer. Freud had argued the need to move beyond a phylogenetic to an ontogenetic explanation; for Fanon, what was required was a sociogenic explanation. Although *Black Skin, White Masks* would have a second life as a central text in the postmodern canon, thirty years after it was published, the book was in no way a call to identity politics. Quite the contrary, as Fanon's lines in the concluding pages make clear:

> The disaster of the man of color lies in the fact that he was enslaved. The disaster and inhumanity of the white man lie in the fact that somewhere he has killed man.
> And even today they subsist, to organize this dehumanization rationally. But I as a man of color, to the extent that it becomes possible for me to exist absolutely, do not have the right to lock myself into a world of retroactive reparations.
>
> I, the man of color, want only this:
> That the tool never possesses the man. That the enslavement of man by man cease forever; that is, of one by another. That it may become possible for me to discover and to love man, wherever he may be. The Negro is not. Any more than the white man.[38]

Whatever Fanon was, he was not a postmodernist. He might rather be characterized as one part Marxist Freudian, one part Freudian Marxist, and most part totally committed to revolutionary liberation movements. If he belonged to his time, however, his work still has much to offer ours. The very last sentence of *Black Skin, White Masks* is this: "My final prayer: O my body, make of me always a man who questions!" It is in this spirit of interrogation that I offer my reflections on the utility of Fanon's thought for the twenty-first century.

I am struck, on rereading his books, firstly by the degree to which they make very strong declarations of which Fanon seems entirely confident, especially when he is being critical of others; and secondly, by the way these declarations are usually followed, sometimes many pages later, by Fanon spelling out his uncertainties about how best to proceed, how to achieve what needs to be accomplished. I am also struck, as was Sartre, by the degree to which these books are not at all addressed to the powerful of the world but rather to the "wretched of the earth," a category that overlaps heavily for him with "people of color." Fanon is always angry at the powerful, who are both cruel and condescending. But he is even angrier at those people of color whose behavior and attitudes contribute to sustaining the world of inequality and humiliation, and who often do so merely to obtain crumbs for themselves. In what follows, I will organize my reflections around what I think are three dilemmas for Fanon—the use of violence, the assertion of identity and the class struggle.

What gave *The Wretched of the Earth* so much punch and attracted so much attention—both of admiration and of condemnation—was the opening sentence of the first chapter, "Concerning Violence":

> National liberation, national renaissance, the restoration of nationhood to the people, commonwealth: whatever may be the headings used or the new formulas introduced, decolonization is always a violent phenomenon.[39]

Is this an analytical observation or a policy recommendation? The answer may be that it is meant to be both. Perhaps Fanon himself is not sure which of the two meanings takes priority; and perhaps it does not matter. The idea that fundamental social change never occurs without the use of force was not a new one. All the radical emancipatory traditions of the nineteenth century had believed that the privileged never cede real power voluntarily; power is always wrenched from them. This belief helped define the presumed difference between a "revolutionary" and a "reformist" path to social change. Yet in the post-1945 period, the utility of the distinction between "revolution" and "reform" was wearing thin—wearing thin among the very militants of the most impatient, angry, uncompromising movements. And therefore, the use of violence, not as sociological analysis but as policy recommendation, was coming into question.

If "revolutionary" movements, once in power, seemed to accomplish much less than they had promised, it was equally true that "reformist" movements did not do much better. Hence the ambivalence about the policy on violence. Algerian nationalists had lived through this cycle in their own biographical experience. Ferhat Abbas, president of the GPRA from its foundation in 1958 to 1961, had spent the first thirty years of his political life as a reformist, only to admit that he and his movement had got nowhere. He concluded that violent uprising was the only meaningful tactic if Algeria did not wish to be forever a colony, and "enslaved."

In *Wretched of the Earth*, Fanon seems to be making three points about the use of force as a political tactic. First of all, in the

"Manichean" colonial world, its original source is located in the continuing violent acts of the colonizer:

> He of whom *they* have never stopped saying that the only language he understands is that of force decides to give utterance by force. In fact, as always, the settler has shown him the way he should take if he is to become free. The argument the colonized person chooses has been furnished by the settler, and by an ironic turning of the tables, it is the colonized person who now affirms that the colonialist understands nothing but force.[40]

The second point is that this violence transforms both the social psychology and the political culture of those who were colonized.

> But it so happens that for the colonized people this violence, because it constitutes their only work, invests their characters with positive and creative qualities. The practice of violence binds them together as a whole, since each individual forms a link in the great chain, a part of the great organism of violence which has surged upwards in reaction to the settler's violence in the beginning. The groups recognize each other and the future nation is already indivisible. The armed struggle mobilizes the people; that is to say, it throws them in one way and one direction.[41]

The third point, however, seems to contradict the optimistic tone of the second, the seemingly irreversible path towards national and human liberation evoked in the opening chapter. The second and third chapters of the book, written during the ongoing war for national liberation in Algeria, are particularly fascinating for the light they throw on "Concerning Violence." The second chapter, "Spontaneity: Its Strengths and Weaknesses," is a generalized critique of nationalist movements. Their "inherent defect," Fanon says, is their focus on "those elements which are the most politically conscious: the working classes in the towns, the skilled workers and the civil servants"—that is to say, a tiny portion of the population, which hardly represents more than 1 percent:

> The overwhelming majority of nationalist parties show a deep distrust towards the people of the rural areas.... The Westernized elements experience feelings with regard to the bulk of the peasantry which are reminiscent of those found among the town workers of industrialized countries.[42]

This inherent defect is precisely what makes them fail to be revolutionary movements, which cannot be based on a Westernized proletariat but must rely rather on the uprooted peasantry, blocked on the outer fringe of the urban centers:

> It is within this mass of humanity, this people of the shanty towns, at the core of the lumpenproletariat that the rebellion will find its urban spearhead. For the lumpenproletariat, that horde of starving men, uprooted from their tribe and from their clan, constitutes one of the most spontaneous and the most radically revolutionary forces of a colonized people.[43]

Fanon passes from this paean to the detribalized lumpenproletariat to an analysis of the nature of nationalist movements once in power. He is ferocious and unforgiving, and denounces them in one of the most famous sentences in this book: "The single party is the modern form of the dictatorship of the bourgeoisie, unmasked, unpainted, unscrupulous and cynical." The national bourgeoisie of underdeveloped countries "should not be opposed because it threatens to slow down the total, harmonious development of the nation," he declares. "It should simply be stoutly opposed because, literally, it is good for nothing." He then proceeds to a denunciation of nationalism, pure and simple:

> Nationalism is not a political doctrine, nor a program. If you really wish your country to avoid regression, or at best halts and uncertainties, a rapid step must be taken from national consciousness to political and social consciousness.... A bourgeoisie that provides nationalism alone as food for the masses fails in its mission and gets caught up in a whole series of mishaps.[44]

It is at this point that Fanon turns to the question of identity, my second theme. He initiates the discussion by saying that, of course, vaunting ancient civilizations does not feed anyone today. But it serves the legitimate purpose of taking a distance from Western culture. The racialization of culture was the responsibility initially of the colonizers, "those Europeans who have never ceased to set up white culture to fill the gap left by the absence of other cultures." The concept of Negritude, Fanon argues, "was the emotional if not the logical antithesis of that insult which the white man flung at humanity." But, he goes on, "this historical obligation which has brought the men of African culture to racialize their claims ... will tend to lead them up a blind alley." Fanon is very critical of any attempt to assert cultural identity that is independent of, not located within, the political struggle for national liberation. In the fourth chapter, "On National Culture," he writes:

> To believe that it is possible to create a black culture is to forget that Negroes are disappearing.... There will never be such a thing as black culture because there is not a single politician who feels he has a vocation to bring black republics into existence. The problem is to get to know the place that these men mean to give their people, the kind of social relations that they decide to set up and the conception they have of the future of humanity. It is this that counts; everything else is mystification, signifying nothing.[45]

His closing thrust is quite the opposite of identity politics:

> If man is known by his acts, then we will say that the most urgent thing today for the intellectual is to build his nation. If this building is true, that is, if it interprets the manifest will of the people and reveals the eager African peoples, then the building of a nation is of necessity accompanied by the discovery and encouragement of universalizing values. Far from keeping aloof from other nations, therefore, it is national liberation which leads the nation to play its part on the stage of history. It is at the heart of national consciousness that international consciousness lives and grows. And this twofold emerging is ultimately only the source of all culture.[46]

In the Conclusion to *Wretched of the Earth*, however, as though he had gone too far in understating the merits of a different path for Africa—a non-European path—Fanon points to the example of the United States, which had made as its goal that of catching up with Europe, and succeeded so well that it "became a monster, in which the taints, the sickness and the inhumanity of Europe have grown to appalling dimensions." For Fanon, then, Africa must not try to "catch up" and become a third Europe. Quite the contrary:

> Humanity is waiting for something other from us than such an imitation, which would be almost an obscene caricature. If we want to turn Africa into a new Europe and America into a new Europe, then let us leave the destiny of our countries to Europeans. They will know

> how to do it better than the most gifted from among us. But if we want humanity to advance a step further, if we want to bring it up to a different level than that which Europe has shown it, then we must invent and we must make discoveries.... For Europe, for ourselves and for humanity, comrades, we must turn over a new leaf, we must work out new concepts, and try to set afoot a new man.[47]

In Fanon's weaving, in both books, around the question of cultural identity, of national identity, we see the fundamental dilemma that has plagued all antisystemic thought in the last half-century and probably in the next as well. The rejection of European universalism is fundamental to the rejection of pan-European dominance and its rhetoric of power in the structure of the modern world-system—what Aníbal Quijano has termed the coloniality of power. But, at the same time, all those who have been committed to the struggle for an egalitarian world, or to what might be called the historic socialist aspiration, are very wary of what Fanon called the "pitfalls of national consciousness." So we continue to weave, for to do so seems the only way to remain on a path to a future in which, in Fanon's words, humanity "advances a step further."

My third theme, the class struggle, is never centrally discussed as such anywhere in Fanon's writings. And yet it is central to his world-view and to his analyses. For, of course, Fanon was brought up in a Marxist culture—in Martinique, in France, in Algeria. The language he knew and that of all those he worked with was impregnated with Marxist premises and vocabulary. But at the same time, Fanon and those he worked with had rebelled, forcefully, against the ossified Marxism of the Communist movements of his era. Aimé Césaire's *Discourse on Colonialism* remains the classic expression of why intellectuals of the colonial world (and of course not they alone) withdrew their commitment to Communist parties and asserted a revised version of the class struggle. The key issue in these debates was the question, which are the classes that are struggling? For a long time, the discussion was dominated by the categories of the German Social Democratic Party and the Communist Party of the Soviet Union. The basic argument was that, in a modern capitalist world, the two classes that were in fundamental conflict and dominated the scene were the urban, industrial bourgeoisie and the urban, industrial proletariat. All other groupings were remnants of dead or dying structures and were destined to disappear, as everyone came to blend into, define themselves as, bourgeois and proletarian.

By the time Fanon was writing, relatively few people regarded this as an adequate or reliable summary of the real situation. The urban industrial proletariat was nowhere near a majority of the world's population and in general, did not seem to be a group that had nothing to lose but its chains. As a result, most movements and intellectuals were in search of a different framing of the class struggle that fitted better as sociological analysis and served more effectively as the basis of radical politics. There were many proposals of new candidates for the historical subject who would be the "spearhead" of revolutionary activity. Fanon thought he had located them in the detribalized, urbanized, lumpenproletariat. But he admitted his doubts when he depicted the "pitfalls of spontaneity."

In the end, what we have from Fanon is more than passion and more than a blueprint for political action. He offers a brilliant delineation of our collective dilemmas. Without violence the wretched of the earth can accomplish nothing. But violence, however therapeutic and however effective, solves nothing. Without breaking from the domination of pan-European culture, it is impossible to move forward. But the consequent assertion of particularity is stultifying and leads inevitably to "pitfalls." The class struggle is central, provided we know which are the classes that are really struggling. But lumpenclasses, on their own, without organizational structure, burn out.

We find ourselves, as Fanon expected, in the long transition from our existing capitalist world-system to something else. It is a struggle whose outcome is totally uncertain. Fanon might not have said so, but his books are evidence that he sensed it. Whether we can emerge collectively from this struggle and into a better world-system is in large part dependent on our ability to confront the three dilemmas discussed by Fanon—to confront them, and to deal with them in a way that is simultaneously analytically intelligent, morally committed to the "disalienation" for which Fanon fought, and politically adequate to the realities we face.

NOTES

1. In addition, South Africa had a mandate in Southwest Africa, and the legal status of the erstwhile Italian colonies was about to be decided as part of the postwar settlement.

2. The nearest thing is in the Declaration of the Colonial Peoples: "The peoples of the colonies must have the right to elect their own Governments, without restrictions from foreign Powers." Appendix in Colin Legum, *Pan-Africanism: A Short Political Guide* (New York: Praeger, 1962), p. 137.

3. United Kingdom, Colonial Office, Gold Coast: *Report to His Excellency the Governor by the Committee on Constitutional Reform, 1949*, Colonial No. 250, London: HMSO, 1949, Appendix XIV, 100-104.

4. Kwame Nkrumah, *Neo-Colonialism: The Last Stage of Imperialism* (Edinburgh: Thomas Nelson, 1965).

5. Julius K. Nyerere, *Freedom and Unity* (London: Oxford University Press, 1967), 205, 208. This is a talk first given to a world youth conference in 1962 and repeated in expanded form to the Afro-Asian Solidarity Conference in Moshi on 4 February 1963.

6. See Tables 11 and 13 in The World Bank, *World Development Report, 1979* (New York: Oxford University Press, 1979), pp. 11 and 13.

7. For a discussion of the theoretical problems of measuring this, with some data from the United States and southern Africa, see Immanuel Wallerstein, William G. Martin, and Torry Dickinson, "Household Structures and Production Processes: Preliminary Theses and Findings," *Review*, v, 3, Winter 1982, 437-458.

8. Michael F. Lofchie, "Political and Economic Origins of African Hunger," *Journal of Modern African Studies*, XIII, 4 December 1975, 554.

9. See Nicole Ball, "Understanding the Causes of African Famine," *Journal of Modern African Studies*, XIV, 3 September 1976, 517-522; R. W. Franke and B. H. Chasin, *Seeds of Famine: Ecological Destruction and the Development Dilemma in the West African Sahel* (Montclair, N.J.: Allanheld, Osmun & Co.,

1980); Comité d'Information Sahel, *Qui se nourrit de la famine en Afrique?* (Paris: Maspero, 1975).

10. See chapter 1 of my *Historical Capitalism* (London: New Left Books, 1983).

11. See chapter 3 of ibid.

12. This essay was co-authored with William G. Martin.

13. This article was the keynote address at the Annual Meeting of the South African Sociological Association, Durban, South Africa, July 7-11, 1996.

14. For an elaboration of these ideas, see "The French Revolution as a World-Historical Event," in *Unthinking Social Science*, Polity Press, Cambridge, 1991, pp 7-22.

15. The argument in the following paragraphs summarizes an extensive analysis in Terence K Hopkins and Immanuel Wallerstein, coordinators, *The Age of Transition: Trajectory of the World-System, 1945-2025*, forthcoming, Zed Press, 1996.

16. See Fernand Braudel, *Capitalism and Civilisation, 15th to 18th Century*, 3 Volumes, Harper and Row, New York, 1981-84.

17. Keynote address for conference on "Ethnic Labels, Signs of Class: The Construction and Implications of Collective Identity," October 11-12, 1985, sponsored by Center for Study of Industrial Societies, University of Chicago.

18. See Immanuel Wallerstein, *Historical Capitalism*. London: New Left Books, 1983, pp. 19-26; idem, "Household structures in the capitalist world-economy." In J. Smith, I. Wallerstein, and H.-D. Evers (eds.), *Households and the World-Economy*. Beverly Hills, CA: Sage, 1984, pp. 17-22.

19. Keynote address at conference, "Development Challenges for the 21st Century," Cornell University, Oct. 1, 2004.

20. Volume III of *Les colonies françaises*, Exposition Universelle de 1900, Publications de la Commission chargée de préparer la participation de la Ministère des Colonies, Paris: Augustin Challamel, 1900.

21. See, for example, Anthony Atkinson, Lee Rainwater & Timothy Smeeding, "Income Distribution in European Countries," in A. B. Atkinson, ed., *Incomes and the Welfare State: Essays on Britain and Europe*. Cambridge: Cambridge University Press, 1995.

22. The classic article is that by Giovanni Arrighi & lessica Drangel, "The Stratification of the World-Economy: An Exploration of the Semiperipheral Zone," *Review*, X, 1, Summer 1986, 9-74. Arrighi is currently updating this argument in a forthcoming article.

23. Although this is prima facie logical, it seldom enters into analyses of mainstream economists.

24. See Deane Neubauer, "Mixed Blessings of the Megacities," *Yale Global Online*, Sept. 24, 2004. <http://yaleglobal.yale.edu/display.article?id=4573>

25. See Ilya Prigogine, in collaboration with Isabelle Stengers, *The End of Certainty: Time, Chaos, and the New Laws of Nature*. New York: Free Press, 1997.

26. See for example "Japan and the Future Trajectory of the World-System: Lessons from History?" in *Geopolitics and Geo-culture*. Cambridge: Cambridge University Press, 1991, 36-48.

27. Keynote address at the University of Vermont, *Rethinking Political Economy: Class, Race, Gender, Nation*, A Conference in Honor of Joan Smith's Contribution to Scholarship, Nov. 10-11, 2006.

28. Joan Smith, "We Irish Women: Gender, History, and the World-Economy," *Review*, XVI, 1 (Win. 1993): 10.

29. Smith, "We Irish Women," 10.

30. Ibid.

31. Smith, "We Irish Women," 14.

32. Keynote address at the 30th Annual Conference of the Political Economy of the World-System Section of the American Sociological Association, Macalester College, April 27, 2006.

33. See *After Liberalism*. New York: New Press, 1995, *and The Decline of American Power: The U.S. in a Chaotic World*. New York; New Press, 2003.

34. Basil Davidson. *Can We Write African History?* Los Angeles: African Studies Center, UCLA. Occasional Paper No.1, November, 1965, p. 6.

35. WE, p. 35

36. Walter Rodney, *A History of the Upper Guinea Coast, 1545 to 1800* (Oxford: Clarendon Press, 1970), ix.

37. The words of Francis Jeanson, who wrote the Preface to the original French edition, *Peau noire, masques blancs*.

38. New York 1963, henceforth WE. Translations amended by the author.

39. Fanon, *Black Skin, White Masks*, London [1967] 1970, pp. 164-5.

40. WE, pp. 315-6.

41. WE, p. 84.

42. WE., p. 93.

43. WE, pp. 108-11.

44. Fanon was here obviously influenced by the Battle of Algiers and its role in the Algerian revolution. WE, p. 129.

45. Respectively, WE, pp. 165, 175-6, 203-4.
46. WE, pp. 212-4, 234-5.
47. WE, pp. 247-8.

INDEX

absolute terms, 53, 58
academy, 110, 146
Accra, 193
acculturation, 148
accumulating capital, 38, 59, 100, 183
accumulation, 16, 26, 36, 38, 78, 93, 95–96, 170, 177, 179, 183, 191
activists, 122, 139, 152
actors, 10, 13–14, 19, 115, 170
   economic, 174
   independent historical, 124
   ineffective, 114
   political, 5
   social, 98
adjustment mechanisms, 36, 38
African continent, 143–44, 156
African Heritage Studies Association (AHSA), 154–55
African historians, 158, 160, 170
African history, 10, 158–61
African intermediaries, 167–68
African leaders, 153, 171, 167, 170
African liberation, 13, 46–47, 55, 155
African National Congress (ANC), 19–21, 23, 25, 27, 29, 31, 33, 35, 37, 39, 70–71, 74
African nationalism, 8–9, 150, 155
African peoples, 167, 199
Africans, 3, 6, 41–42, 52, 54, 64, 70, 73, 144, 146, 149–52, 158–61, 168, 170, 177–78
   enslaved, 111, 167
   scholars, 3, 149–56, 158
   street intellectuals, 158
   young, 160
African society, 169–70, 172
African states, 3, 42, 51, 53, 55–57, 74
African Studies Association (ASA), 151, 153–55
African universities, 152, 159
Africa's struggles, 157
Afrikaner, white, 15, 73
Afro-Asian Solidarity Conference, 202
Afro-Europeans, 170, 173
Afro-pessimism, 42
agency, 166, 170
Aimé Césaire, 193
Alex La Guma, 71–72
Algeria, 10, 33, 43, 47–49, 51, 137, 193, 196–97, 200
Algerian students, 134
alliances, 17, 46, 104, 115, 129–30
   political, 19, 70, 115
ambassadors, 187, 193
Americas, 48, 179, 199
analysis
   intellectual, 91, 178
   political, 117, 120
   sociological, 196, 201
antagonisms, 49, 188
   racial, 180
anthropologists, 112, 148–51, 169
   pre-1950, 152
anthropology, 71, 147–48, 150
antisystemic, 9, 49, 101
   movements, 9–11, 14, 23, 27–29, 32, 34–36, 40, 48, 95, 122, 135, 162
   organized activity, 9–11, 17

INDEX

apartheid, 20, 43, 55, 70, 72, 75
Arab world, 61
archaeologists, 113, 151
armed struggle, 20, 48
arms, 52, 188
Asia, 6–7, 27, 53, 62, 88, 126, 129
assertion, 5, 61, 78, 120, 131, 144, 195
asymptote, 36, 100
Atlantic slave trade, 169, 172–73. *See also* slavery
autonomy, 24, 41, 48
banks, 52, 56, 89
Bantus, 69–70
battle, 13, 83, 113, 119, 204
   political, 19, 60
belief, 24, 29–30, 44–45, 48, 64–65, 88, 116, 196
Bharatiya Janata Party (BJP), 137
bifurcation, 39, 60, 103
blacks, 69, 74, 111, 119, 154–55, 173
borders, 105
boundaries, 112, 115
bourgeoisie, 198
Brazil, 90, 105, 136, 152
Britain, 14, 203
   hegemony, 15–16
Buddhists, 131, 133
cadres, 28–29, 33, 61–62, 95
Canada, 88, 123, 152
Cancun, 90, 105
capital, 26, 36, 38, 59, 90, 95–96, 100, 119, 170, 174, 176, 179, 182–83, 185, 191
   accumulation, 15, 18, 96, 103, 178
capitalism, 39, 85, 95–96, 104, 106, 166, 171, 179–87, 190–92, 203
   analysis of, 182, 190
      European, 171
      historical, 28, 85, 179, 202–3
capitalist economies, 183–84, 186–87, 189
capitalist nations, 183, 185, 187–88
capitalists, 6, 36–39, 100, 163, 174–75, 178, 181, 184, 188, 190
capitalist system., 83, 170–71, 180, 183–85, 187–88. *See also* capitalism

capitalist world, 175, 180
capitalist world economy, 8–9, 14, 47, 58–59, 78, 80, 83, 85–86, 92–95, 97–101, 103, 143–44, 179, 183, 185–86
capitalization, 118–19
caste, 180, 192
categories, 64, 70–71, 73, 76–77, 80, 83, 93, 110–11, 113, 120, 127, 195, 200
   genetic, 77, 80
   racial, 80, 110
Catholics, 118, 125
Central America, 5, 7
centrality, 109–11, 127, 137, 187–88
chains, commodity, 16, 47, 79
chaos, 39, 203
China, 10, 21, 25, 45, 48, 81, 92, 112
Chinese, 92, 112, 177
Christian churches, 28, 126–28, 187
Christianity, 126, 131, 134–35, 137, 143–44, 169
cities, 63, 97, 190
civilizing mission, 27, 88
class conflict, 109
classes, 6, 15, 78, 85, 109–10, 115, 120, 122, 124, 156, 180, 188, 192, 200–201, 203–4
   dangerous, 27, 58, 96, 99, 101
   planter, 178, 181
   popular, 58
   working, 166, 172, 174, 177, 188, 197
class struggle, 6, 11, 97, 106, 166, 180, 188, 195, 200–201
cloth, 168–69
coalition, 105, 138–39
Cold War, 45, 57, 127–30
collaboration, 139, 203
colonial governments, 47, 149–50, 178
colonialism, 4–5, 13, 41, 47, 171–72, 200
colonial rule, 150–51, 172, 197–98
colonies, 82, 87, 149, 196, 202–3
color, 80, 110, 117, 181, 187, 195
"colored people," 111, 118

INDEX

Coloured, 71–73, 75
  people, 69–77
    oppressed, 74–75
    word, 72
communism, 54, 57–58, 88, 128, 130
communist world, 49, 127
communities, 84, 113, 184, 188
competition, 83, 93
  international, 177, 188
comrades, 69, 200. *See also* cadres
concessions, 11, 30–31, 38, 96, 99, 168, 174
conditions, 16–20, 75, 94, 106, 175, 178
  structural, 14, 170
conflict, 6, 13–14, 105–6
Congo, 13, 47
  crisis, 42, 46–47
consciousness, national, 61, 198–200
constitutional reform, 3, 202
constraints, 21, 79, 101–2, 127, 146, 149–50, 170
contention, 119, 134, 171, 177
contest, 5, 15, 59, 103, 113
continuum, 6, 148, 175
contradictions, 10, 12, 57, 79, 85–86, 121, 145
  basic, 37, 85
control, 8, 14, 18, 26, 32, 48, 52, 57, 79, 144, 154, 160, 170, 175, 185
controversies, 117, 160
core areas, 15–17, 50, 83
  overseas, 17
core-periphery relationships, 17, 78–79, 83, 171, 179, 185
corporate takeovers, 56, 58
corporations, 20, 51, 56
corruption, 33, 52, 62
costs, 37–38, 50, 54, 84, 88–89, 96–100, 130, 175
  collective, 98–99
  externalization of, 37, 98
  internalization of, 38, 98, 100
  of production, 37, 50, 98–100
  rising, 18, 100

countries, 7, 9, 11, 33–34, 53–55, 74–75, 88–89, 91–94, 102, 105–6, 112, 126–27, 185, 188, 198–99
  backward, 182, 185–86
  particular, 46, 162
  underdeveloped, 166, 198
Cox, Oliver, 179–80, 192
crime, 6, 42
crisis, 36, 39, 60, 64, 145, 155
  debt, 50, 55, 57
  ecological, 37–38
  systemic, 145
Crusades, 134
Cuba, 48
  Communist Party, 47
cultivation, 8, 79
culture contact, 150
cultures, 29, 84, 148–50, 191, 198–99
  black, 199
  political, 106, 197
cutbacks, 100
cynicism, 4, 11, 41
Dakar (Senegal), 41
Davidson, Basil, 42, 157–61, 163, 204
debt, 54–55, 58, 158
decolonization, 8, 10, 13, 19, 26, 46–48, 196
defeat, 43, 157, 174
defect, inherent, 197–98
demands, 38, 60, 62, 99–100, 105–6, 111, 127, 154, 185
democracy, 45, 59, 128, 144
democratization, 38, 58–60, 62, 155
Denmark, 81, 91–92, 94, 106, 124
dependencies, 88, 166
de-ruralization, 36–37, 97
detoxification, 98
development, 14, 18–19, 21, 53–54, 57, 59–60, 79–80, 82, 87–91, 93, 102–3, 124, 180, 183, 186
  economic, 44, 58, 87–88, 94, 177, 191
  national, 34, 48
  positive, 23, 36
developmentalism, 87–91, 93, 95, 97, 99, 101, 103, 105, 107

209

INDEX

dictatorships, 42, 198
difficulties, economic, 18, 52, 57
disarray, 60–62, 64
disaster, 195
discourse, 126–27, 130
diseases, 4, 42
disillusionment, 11, 34, 49, 57–58, 95, 101, 130, 162
disintegration, 39, 55, 62
distribution, 51, 80, 93–94, 103
diversification, 16, 184
division, 6, 36, 45, 139, 147
domains, 100, 102, 147
   normal, 151
domination, 25, 185–86, 201
earth, 194, 196, 199, 201
East Asia, 54, 58
economic activities, 16, 20
economists, 109, 147, 151
egalitarian, 59, 104, 140, 200
Egypt, 3, 24, 81
election, 59, 80, 155
electoral contests, 105, 116
elites, 52, 130
enemies, 73, 119, 135–36
energy, nuclear, 138
Enlightenment, 12, 153, 161–62
enterprises, productive, 26, 93, 107
entities, 81, 85, 114, 148
   political, 82–83
environment, 122, 130, 148
equality, 44, 59, 117, 121, 157, 170
era, colonial, 41, 87
establishment, 16, 78, 82
estate, 175–77
Ethiopia, 3, 81
ethnic groups, 73, 76–78, 83–85, 110–11
ethnicity, 84, 116, 118
ethnicization, 84–85
ethnocentrism, 150, 153
Europe, 9, 27, 41, 45, 49, 80, 88, 125–26, 170–72, 182, 190, 199–200, 203
   eastern, 45, 57–58, 123
   new, 199
   southeastern, 126
Europeans, 43, 69–70, 73, 87, 126, 144, 146, 149–50, 153, 157, 168–69, 171–73, 198–99
European states, 3, 126
European Union, 38, 105, 126, 128
evolution, 79, 115, 147–48, 167–68
exchange, 76, 139, 167
expansion, 8, 20, 39, 56, 58, 79, 166, 169
   economic, 20–21
   enormous, 18, 100
expenditures, 38, 52, 55, 98–100
   military, 56, 182
exploitation, 88, 166, 172
exports, 7, 15, 51, 53, 55, 89, 168, 172, 189
   crops, 8
failures, 23, 34, 36, 38, 57, 96, 129–30, 132, 139, 162
faith, 32, 41, 44, 101
famines, 7–8, 55, 202
feminists, 117–18
feudalism, 183
fiscal crises, 38, 63
food, 184, 198
forces, 5, 9–10, 13, 15, 18, 25, 34–35, 39, 46–47, 61, 70, 131, 148, 159, 196–97
   historical, 165
   political, 61, 130
   primary, 136, 150
   regional, 13, 18
   strong, 49, 126
foreign commerce, 184–85, 189
forum, 136, 139
   open, 121, 139
France, 3, 20, 24, 27, 62, 81, 124, 126, 134, 193, 200
freedom, 3–4, 157, 175, 185, 202
Freedom Charter, 70–71
French Revolution, 23, 203
Front de Liberation National (FLN), 134
fundamentalisms, 128, 131, 133, 135–37, 139

INDEX

fundamentalist movements, 111, 132
GDP, 7, 92
gender, 110, 113, 115, 117–20, 122, 124, 132, 204
geo-culture, 23, 26, 31, 35, 44, 49, 58, 203
geopolitical arena, 21, 46, 54, 102
Germany, 43, 81, 89
Ghana, 3, 42, 49, 193
ghettos, 113
globalization, 89–91, 93–95, 97, 99, 101, 103, 105, 107, 121
gold, 59, 177
Gouvernement Provisoire de la République Algérienne (GPRA), 193, 196
governments, 4, 47, 50, 53–54, 56, 58, 70–73, 82, 98–101, 104–6, 109, 127, 133, 151, 175
  progressive, 106, 154
Great Britain, 3, 24, 43, 54, 128
Greece, 24, 81
groups, 49–50, 53, 60, 62, 69–72, 82, 84, 110–19, 121–23, 138–39, 153, 155, 170, 172–73, 177
  naming, 109, 111, 113, 115, 117, 119, 121, 123
  small, 28–30, 53, 113, 167
  weaker, 60, 120
growth, 7, 23, 54, 151, 169, 171, 183
  economic, 92, 106–7
  rates of, 53, 92
Guyana, 174, 176–77
health, 90, 99, 122
hegemony, 18–19, 26, 49
hierarchy, 115, 121, 170, 175
Hindu, 131, 133, 137
hinterland, 169, 177
historians, 27, 82, 147, 150–51, 165
historical
  subjects, 119, 201
  system, 39, 64, 76, 78–79, 85–86, 96
  trajectories, 7–8

history, 8–9, 25, 27, 29–30, 32–33, 69–70, 115, 119–20, 124–25, 158–59, 161, 165, 169–70, 178, 203–4
  economic, 181, 191
Holland, 189–90
Holy Roman Empire, 81, 126
homogeneous, 73, 80, 110
hospitals, 63, 106, 194
hostility, 33–34
household, structures, 78, 84, 202–3
households, 84, 97, 120, 177, 203
humanity, 42, 198–200
Hussein, Saddam, 135
hypocrisy, 115
identities, 72, 85, 109, 111, 119–21, 124, 194–95, 198
  cultural, 31, 199–200
  national, 27, 124, 200
identity politics, 70, 72, 74, 76, 78, 80, 82, 84, 86, 88, 90, 92, 94, 96, 122–24
ideological struggle, 45
ideologies, 44, 49, 58, 82, 88, 132, 138, 161
  dominant, 58, 144
ignorance, 158, 184
imbalance, 174, 186
IMF policies, 55–56
imperialism, 3, 18, 121, 139, 186–87, 202
imports, 7, 14, 16, 55, 89, 114, 175–76, 189
incapacity, 36, 49
inclusion, 64, 110
income, 7, 52, 91, 130, 203
  national, 54, 188
  real, 7–8, 53, 59, 92, 97
indentured labor, 175–76
independence, 3–9, 11, 26, 42, 49, 51, 172, 193
  movements, 5, 10, 47
India, 26, 81, 105, 123, 137, 152
Indian National Congress, 25
Indians, 69–70, 73–75, 177–78
industrialization, 44, 183

INDEX

import-substitution, 88–89
industrialized countries, 7, 197
inegalitarian world-system, 91, 94
inequality, 85, 121, 195
infrastructure, 52, 55, 57, 98–99
  physical, 63
inhumanity, 195, 199
inputs, 16, 40, 96–98, 102
institutions, 84, 106, 135
  cultural, 91
  religious, 127
integration, 124, 169
intellectuals, 43, 61, 88, 200–201
International Congress of Africanists, 155
interstate system, 6, 14–15, 18–19, 31, 78, 81–83, 162, 187–88
inventions, 78, 115, 132, 180
investment, 57, 130, 190
Iran, 48, 51, 81, 137–38
Iraq, 51, 90, 135
Ireland, 24, 124
Islam, 125–27, 129, 131, 133, 135, 137, 139, 143, 169
Islamist groups, 43, 125, 133, 135–36, 138
Islamist movements, 137
Italy, 24, 62, 81, 92, 157
Japan, 18, 21, 46, 49, 53–54, 57–59, 62, 81, 124, 152, 203
  and East Asia, 102–3
Jews, 69, 131, 134, 143
jihad, 169
Judaism, 143
judgment, 115, 189
  moral, 114–15, 124
Kenya, 48, 113
kings, 167, 172
knowledge, 28, 160
  scientific, 44, 145
labels, 69–70, 72, 80, 123
  legal, 70
labor, 15–16, 36–37, 79, 83–84, 128, 176–77, 185, 187
  axial division of, 78–80, 179, 185
  division of, 37, 79, 169, 185
  field, 176
  free wage, 174
  global division of, 15–16
  part-time, 177
  village, 175–77
laborers, 83, 176–77
  village, 175
lançados, 167
land, 43, 177–78, 190
language, 44, 60, 88, 111–12, 117, 197, 200
Latin America, 27, 49, 53, 55, 58, 61–62, 88, 123, 129, 191
laws, 69–70, 80, 85, 131
  customary, 168
leaders, 19, 26, 28–29, 32, 72, 189, 193
leadership, 4–5, 29, 32, 179, 185–86, 188, 190, 194
leftists, 45, 135
legitimacy, 23, 30, 39, 85, 131, 150–51, 154, 169
legitimation, 27, 48, 62, 82, 85
lending, 52, 55
liberalism, 27, 58, 204
liberal mediators, 149–50, 152–55
liberation, 23, 25, 48
  human, 35, 197
  movements, 23, 26–27, 32, 39, 154
  wars, 48, 158
Liberia, 3, 31, 62
loans, 53–54, 89–90
logic, 95, 129, 138, 143
magic, 34, 59
maladies, 4
Mande, 169, 172
market, 34, 37, 50, 58–59, 90, 175, 184–86
Martinique, 193, 200
Marxism, 44, 58, 85, 109, 135, 144, 180, 183, 191
mass, 28, 31–33, 39, 101, 131, 135, 198
  mobilization, 29
  support, 28, 30, 61
media, 28, 119
mercantilism, 188–89
Mexico, 25, 55, 89, 124

INDEX

Middle East, 20, 125–26
middle strata, 53, 62
militants, 3, 196
military, 13, 15
minority, 75–76, 83, 136
missionaries, 148, 150
mobilization, 9, 29, 31, 33, 60–61
models, 31, 54
modernism, 36, 48, 132–33
money, 38–39, 52, 55–56, 58, 63, 89
monopolies, 93, 105, 127, 169, 184
Morocco, 81–82
movements, 20–21, 23–26, 28–34, 38–40, 48, 60–62, 81, 95, 101, 106, 121–23, 129–40, 157–58, 162–63, 193–94
    communist, 61, 126, 129, 200
    fundamentalist, 136–38
    indigenist, 136
    left, 135, 137
    multiple, 24, 104
    religious, 132–33, 139
    revolutionary, 95, 196, 198
    social democratic, 61, 129
Mozambique, 10, 13
Muslim populations, 131, 134, 136–37
Muslims, 125, 131, 134, 169
myth, 73, 81
nationalism, 69, 82–83, 132, 135, 188, 198
nationality, 118, 149
national liberation, 13–15, 23, 26, 28, 58, 74, 124, 127, 196–97, 199
    movements, 23–26, 28, 34–36, 39, 41, 45, 47–49, 60–62, 81, 127, 129–31, 150, 152, 193–94, 197–98
national minorities, 73–77
nationhood, 83, 196
nations, 23–25, 41, 44, 73–78, 80–83, 85, 110, 113, 120, 122, 182, 185–86, 188–90, 197–99, 204
    leader, 185, 187. *See also* leaders
NATO, 46, 128
Negritude, 152, 198
neocolonialism, 5–6
neo-liberalism, 95, 130, 139, 161

Nigeria, 42, 60
Nkrumah, Kwame, 4–6, 25, 49, 202
nobility, 167, 172–73
non-European world, 47, 87, 126
North America, 16, 49, 62, 123, 145
OECD countries, 91
oil, 51
    prices, 50–52, 54, 89
    producers, 50–51
OPEC, 50–51, 89
opposition, 11, 28, 49, 70, 99, 116, 121, 139
oppression, 28–29, 121, 144–45
optimism, 41, 43, 49, 60, 94
organizations, 5, 10–11, 42, 70, 86, 122–23, 155, 178, 187
    rival, 71, 155
outsiders, 43, 70, 155
pan-European world, 87–88, 129
Paris, 87, 202–3
parties, 26, 59
    communist, 49, 200
passions, 29–30, 76, 137, 140, 157, 201
payments, 54, 97
    difficulties, 18, 53, 89
peace, 13, 126
peasants, 122, 175, 177
pejorative terms, 111, 116–17
people, 3–5, 21, 24–25, 27–28, 44–45, 59–60, 69–73, 75–77, 82, 91, 112–13, 185, 187–88, 195–99, 201–2
    colonized, 197–98
    working, 174–76, 178
peoplehood, 76–78, 84–86
    construction of, 69, 71, 73, 75, 77, 79, 81, 83, 85
peripheral processes, 79
peripheral zones, 12, 16–17, 24, 34, 50–51, 83, 174, 191
periphery, 8, 79, 92, 171–72, 186
personnel, 41, 96, 107, 152
pitfalls, 116, 200–201
plagues, 93, 170
planters, 174–76
Poland, 24, 53, 55, 57, 89

polarization, 8, 79–80, 91, 93, 103–4, 128
  internal, 53, 56
Polisario front, 81–82
political
  debates, 69, 110, 113, 126, 154
  decisions, 41, 45, 144
  economy, 109–10, 123, 204
  issues, 24, 115, 155
  kingdom, 8, 25
  movements, 6, 46, 136, 150
  processes, 79, 172
  strategies, 120, 124
  terms, 21, 134, 149
  turmoil, 23, 153
political structures, 95–96, 101
political struggles, 9, 95, 156, 161, 180, 199
politicians, 61, 94, 121, 128
populations, 7, 28, 31–33, 37, 39, 41, 51, 55–56, 60, 75, 91, 101–2, 127, 131, 167
  world's, 34, 36, 130, 201
Porto Alegre, 90, 95, 103–4, 106, 121
Portugal, 3, 16, 19–20, 81, 92
Portuguese, 173, 177
positions, 3–4, 43, 56, 89, 103, 118, 138–39, 153, 171
  economic, 53, 56
postwar period, 16–17
poverty, 6, 106
power, 4, 6, 12–13, 15–16, 23–27, 29–34, 36, 38–39, 47–48, 61, 101, 137–38, 162, 196, 200
  bargaining, 37, 175
  colonial, 4, 41, 46–47, 149
  great, 45, 48
  movements in, 30–34, 95
  political, 20, 23, 25
  social, 83
prejudice, 170, 187
pressures, 55, 63, 96, 98, 102–3, 144, 175, 177
prestige, 6, 111
Pretoria, 13
prices, 20, 34, 50–51, 176

sales, 100
primordial, 86, 111
privilege, 39, 95, 114, 121, 185
producers, 50, 98–100
production, 16, 18, 46, 50–51, 54–55, 79, 84, 92–93, 96–100, 184
  increased, 56, 168
  mode of, 28, 166
  processes, 79–80, 202
productive, activities, 31, 50, 54, 90, 93
productivity, 92, 94, 175
products, 35, 37, 46, 50, 79, 169, 177, 186
profits, 11, 37, 39, 50, 54, 87–88, 93, 100, 105, 120, 167, 171, 174, 183
  seeking, 50, 130
progress, 44, 49, 59, 126, 145, 153, 160, 184
proletarianization, 44, 178
proletarians, 11, 175, 201
  urban, 37, 174
promises, 5, 18, 32, 34, 41, 57, 101
proponents, 111
prosperity, 44, 91, 190
protection, 27, 64, 130, 167, 169
public norm, 117
race, 76–78, 80, 83, 85, 110, 113, 115, 120, 122, 124, 156, 166, 180–82, 191–92, 204
  issues of, 110
  prejudice, 181
  relations, 181, 192
racial segregation, 71, 177
racism, 69, 73, 80, 83, 159, 161, 180–82
rebellion, 95, 198
reconstruction, 45, 64
rediscovery, 158, 160
reform, 27, 29–30, 196
regimes, 12, 31, 57, 74, 129, 135, 137–38
  ancien, 24, 33
  Bush, 133, 136
region, 14–15, 17, 20–21, 24, 54, 124
reinforcement, 10, 28, 132, 134
rejection, 74–75, 200

popular expression of, 72, 75
relations, political, 186–87
relationship, 17, 57, 79, 145, 150, 166–67, 182, 185, 189–90
  exploitative, 182, 187
  gendered, 124
relegates, 86, 140, 183
religion, 111, 113, 118, 126–27, 135, 143
religious affiliations, 125, 127
religious values, 126, 135
remuneration, 96–97
renewal, 46, 98
repression, 11, 28, 134
resistance., 82, 127, 134, 178. *See also* rebellion
resolutions, 139, 155
resources, 15, 64, 87–88, 98, 181, 190
  primary, 98
revenues, 51–53, 63
revolution, 9, 11, 29–30, 33–34, 49, 94, 162, 184, 193, 196
  worldwide, 34, 49
revolutionaries, 33, 49, 129, 196
rhetoric, 25, 56, 90, 122, 200
Rhodesian settlers, 16, 49
rights, 111, 113–14, 122, 138
risks, 14, 139, 158
rivalry, 58, 188–89
road, 3, 27, 65, 102, 140
Rodney, Walter, 165, 167–78, 204
rolling stone, 29–30, 32–33, 134
Roman Catholic Church, 127
roots, 81, 90, 161
rulers, 98, 126, 133, 167
ruling class, 167, 181
  white, 181
runaway factories, 97–98
Russia, 33, 81, 90
Sahara, 3
Sahrawi nation, 81–82
salient, 12, 26
scene, 9, 43, 109, 147, 156, 200
  political, 69, 137, 156
scholars, 94, 102, 128, 149, 151–53, 159, 180

schools, 90, 132
scope, 158, 184
Seattle, 90, 95
Sechaba, 71–73
Second World War, 18, 151, 193
sectors, leading, 50–51
secular, 100, 133–35, 137–38
  missionaries, 149, 152
  trends, 60, 63, 79
secularization, 126–27, 144
security, 14, 63, 99–100
semi-peripheral zones, 17, 50, 58
sentences, 119, 195, 198
sentiments, 29, 41, 82, 134
separation, 78, 126
sequence, temporal, 170–71
services, 39, 63–64, 171, 173
  governmental, 51, 57
settler, 14, 197
sins, 32–33
skepticism, 105, 183
slavery, 167–70, 173–75, 177, 187
slogans, 11, 61, 126
Smith, Adam, 37, 109, 189, 203–4
Smith, Joan, 119, 124, 204
snake-oil salesmen, 34–35
social
  action, 10, 152, 161–62
  categories, 78, 111
  changes, 10, 170, 196
  composition, 151, 156
  movements, 9, 94, 110, 145. *See also* movements
  processes, 11, 151
  psychology, 10, 197
  realities, 77, 170
  relations, 167, 199
  sciences, 7, 40, 76, 109–10, 112, 115–16, 170
  wage, 38
socialism, 34, 47, 88, 126, 163. *See also* communism
socialist countries, 6, 18, 53, 57, 86, 89, 129
sociology, 147, 151, 181, 192
Solidarność, 12, 55, 57

Somalia, 43, 62
South Africa, 13, 15–21, 23–27, 29, 31, 33, 35, 37, 39, 43, 69–71, 73–75, 80, 84, 202–3
South African, 11, 15–16, 19–20, 35, 69, 73–75, 77
South African Indian Congress (SAIC), 70
South Asia, 20, 49
Southeast Asia, 54, 61, 90
Southern Africa, 13–21, 27, 33, 46–48, 55, 202
Southern African Development Coordination Conference (SADCC), 20
sovereign, 31, 78, 81–82
  states, 3, 5, 31
sovereignty, 24, 30–31, 170–71
Soviet Union, 45–46, 88, 128–29, 194, 200
Spain, 3, 24, 126
speculation, 92, 96
  financial, 96, 128
spokespersons, 30, 122, 165
stagnation, 34, 50, 54, 63, 89, 128, 130
  economic, 8, 17, 34, 50, 52, 57
stakes, 12, 14
standards, reduced, 51, 92
state boundaries, 77, 83
state power, 10–11, 29, 38, 131, 137–38, 162
states, 28–29, 31, 38–39, 43–44, 48–50, 52, 55–56, 58–59, 61–63, 79, 81–85, 88–90, 110–11, 126–27, 131–34
  central, 179, 189
  leading, 32, 188
  modern, 31
  oil-producing, 51–53, 89
  semi-peripheral, 50, 130
  strong, 39, 48
  welfare, 12, 26, 38, 130, 203
state structures, 36, 38–39, 62–63, 131–32, 172
status, colonial, 4
status quo, 30, 34
strains, 62, 184
strangers, 149–50, 167

strata, 7, 61
  upper, 11, 27
  working, 7, 85
stratification, 177, 180, 203
strife, civil, 123
structural
  changes, 94, 119
  crisis, 4, 6, 8, 10, 12, 14, 16, 18, 20, 24, 26, 28, 30, 32, 102–3
  foundations, 14, 17
structures, 19, 21, 35, 46, 63, 65, 76, 110, 122, 145, 155, 166, 200–201
  complex, 10
  economic, 100, 190
struggle, 9–10, 12–15, 19, 21, 24, 28, 61, 71, 74, 103–4, 114–15, 121, 123–24, 162–63, 200–201
students, 69, 151, 153, 158, 193
success, 10–12, 16, 29, 33, 61, 74, 96, 138, 143, 188
  total, 143
Sudan, 3, 137
superpowers, 44, 46
superstructure, political, 78, 83
surplus-value, 36, 53, 56, 83, 92–93
survival, 20, 177
Syria, 81, 135
system, 35, 38–39, 60, 82–83, 85–86, 95–96, 104, 121, 144–45, 162, 174–75, 177, 179–80, 182, 185–92
  existing, 86, 95, 102–3, 121, 129
  present, 12, 104, 107
systemic transitions, 139, 145
tacticians, 29–30
  political, 29–30
tactics, 26, 29–30, 70, 75, 175–76, 188–90, 196
  hard-line, 30
  political, 26, 196
  reformist, 29
  revolutionary, 29
task gangs, independent, 175–76
taxation, 96, 99–100, 130, 178
technology, 99, 171–72
terminology, 73–75, 89, 112, 116–17
terrain, 114–15, 149

contested, 114–15
territorial units, 113, 182, 185, 187–88
terrorism, 123, 133
Third World, 24, 34, 41, 44, 49, 55–56, 58, 161
threat, 37, 82, 105, 133, 188
tides, 31, 34, 189
Toure, Sekou, 160
towns, 35, 177, 197
trade, 172–73, 185, 189
   foreign, 189
   free, 105, 167
trading, slave, 168, 171, 173. *See also* slavery
tradition, 143–44
trajectory, 14–15, 43, 203
transactions, domestic, 186, 189
transformations, 9, 15, 17, 21, 35, 58, 65, 156, 159
   economic, 16, 20–21
   social, 10, 48–49
transition, 39, 65, 86, 102–3, 123, 203
   speedy, 20
trends, long-term, 36–37
triadic struggles, 102–3
tribalism, 42, 148–50, 152, 198
triumph, 26–27, 35, 101
   political, 27, 128
triumphalism, 33, 95
Turkey, 25, 81
uncertainties, 123, 195, 198
unemployment, 18, 50, 55
Union Génératé des Etudiants Algériens (UGEA), 134–35
United Kingdom, 43, 202. *See also* Britain
United Nations, 3, 5, 80, 89
United Provinces, 189–90
United States, 18–21, 43, 49, 88–90, 102–3, 105, 110–12, 124–25, 128–30, 133–34, 136–37, 151, 153–55, 180–82, 194
unity, 72, 202
universalism, 143–44, 146
universities, 106, 152, 154

Upper Guinea Coast, 165, 167, 169–70, 172–73, 178, 204
uprisings, 48, 72
urbanization, 36, 44
values, universal, 44, 46
Venice, 185–86, 189–90
victims, 120, 173
Vietnam, 10, 48–49
violence, 123, 196–97, 201
   use of, 195–96
voices, 34, 181
votes, 43, 59, 117, 128
wage earners, rural, 175, 177
wages, 55, 175–76
war, 8, 13, 43, 45, 49, 82, 93, 197
   civil, 55, 93, 123, 125
   first Gulf, 129, 135
Washington, DC, 90, 194
wave, 10, 19, 48, 74
   next, 18, 20
wealth, 93–94, 130, 183, 190
weapons, 21, 55, 115, 168, 175–77
welfare, 39, 55, 63, 99–100, 188
West Africa, 168–69, 173
Western cultures, 148–49, 152, 198
Western Europe, 18, 21, 24, 46, 52–53, 57–58, 61, 88, 102, 123, 126, 128–29, 160, 166, 171. *See also* Europe
wisdom, 103, 124
women, 110, 113, 118–19
workers, 37–38, 56, 84, 86, 96–97, 122–23, 175
   industrial, 11, 51
   skilled, 92, 185, 197
   wage, 84, 167
work stoppages, 96, 176
World Bank, 53, 202
world capitalism, 36, 124
world economy, 13–21, 31–32, 34, 46, 50, 54–55, 78–80, 89, 93, 97, 123–24, 128, 130, 169, 203–4
   existing capitalist, 12
world history, 124, 190
world population, 37, 97
world powers, 14–15, 18, 45

world production, 26, 50, 100
world's antisystemic movements, 161–62
World Social Forum (WSF), 104, 121–22, 136–39
world surplus-value, 51–52
world system, 3, 5–7, 9, 11, 182, 188, 192
   existing, 10
world-systems analysis, 179, 181–85, 187–91

World Trade Organization (WTO), 90, 103–4
worldviews, 26, 44, 145
World Wars, 15–16, 24, 26, 126, 148, 157
Yalta accord, 57
Yugoslavia, 92, 128, 157
Zaire, 47, 60
Zimbabwe, 13, 15

www.ingramcontent.com/pod-product-compliance
Lightning Source LLC
Chambersburg PA
CBHW071730080526
44588CB00013B/1966